Every Morning: A Triplet Of Thoughts For Every Day In The Year [ed. By W.b.t.]....

Every morning

EVERY MORNING:

𝔄 𝔗𝔯𝔦𝔭𝔩𝔢𝔱 𝔬𝔣 𝔗𝔥𝔬𝔲𝔤𝔥𝔱𝔰

FOR

EVERY DAY IN THE YEAR.

LONDON: WILLIAM TEGG.

LONDON:
PRINTED BY WILLIAM CLOWES AND SONS,
STAMFORD STREET AND CHARING CROSS.

PREFACE.

THE object of this little book is to create associations much more than to encourage mere habits of routine, however good. Routine, in order to be a helping—and in order not to be a hindering—process, must be made subservient to some high and absorbing purpose; some purpose the overflowing vitality of which shall be made all the more serviceable by a slight admixture of the dead weight of routine. The most difficult people in the world to get any good out of are those whose lives are the most perfectly regular and systematic. The most excellent maxims are liable to lose the greater part of their emphasis if merely set forth in order and left, unaided by any special form of enforcement. We learn from statements made by some of "them of old time," and verified constantly since, that unity involves strength, and that converse is unfailingly useful alike to the talkers and the things talked of. These triplets of thoughts may be regarded each of them as the concentrated essence of a

PREFACE.

conversation, especially as the object has been so to arrange the extracts that they shall be kindred rather than repetitious in their expression. Three thoughts will surely suggest or help on a fourth, and thus an association of ideas will speedily be formed, and no one can tell how far the influence of such associations may extend. Some of these thoughts may become so encrusted with meditations of your own, that they shall contribute to the embellishment of your mind, and consequently of your life, a similar beauty—delicate alike in detail and in general effect—to that which moss or fern-covered fragments of rock give to those choice bits of natural scenery which we have all met with, and most of us, I hope, observed with loving care and anxious appreciation.

W. B. T.

JANUARY.

1. *" Remember now thy Creator."*—ECCLESIASTES xii. I.

> " Creator, lover of the whole,
> Our prayer for body and for soul,
> O hear ; invigorate and control,
> Within us move."—
>
> > *Lynch.*

" It is scarcely too much to say, that every object in nature, animate or inanimate, is in some manner beautiful, so largely has the Creator provided for our pleasures through the sense of sight."— *McCulloch.*

2. *" I am the Lord thy God, the Holy One of Israel, thy Saviour."*— ISAIAH xliii. 3.

> " Thy promise, like an evening breeze,
> Doth fold my leaves in sleep ;
> Who trusts, the Lord will surely guard,
> Who loves, the Lord will keep."—
>
> > *Williams.*

" Conviction, were it never so excellent, is worthless till it convert itself into conduct. Nay, properly, conviction is not possible till then."—*Carlyle.*

3. *" I will not fail thee, nor forsake thee."*—JOSHUA i. 5.

> " Oh ! I have seen the day,
> When with a single word,
> God helping me to say,
> ' My trust is in the Lord,'
> My soul hath quelled a thousand foes,
> Fearless of all that could oppose."—
>
> > *Cowper.*

" When men cease to be faithful to their God, he who expects to find them so to each other will be much disappointed."—*Horne.*

4. *" Christ Jesus came into the world to save sinners."*—
1 TIMOTHY i. 15.

" Forget not yet the tried intent
Of such a truth as I have meant ;
My great travail so gladly spent
Forget not yet !"—

Wyat.

" Nobody is exceedingly wicked all at once : the devil is too cunning to startle men."—*Bishop Wilson.*

---

5. *" Wait on the Lord : be of good courage, and He shall strengthen thine heart."*—PSALM xxvii. 14.

" How happy is he born and taught,
That serveth not another's will ;
Whose armour is his honest thought,
And simple truth his utmost skill !"—

Wotton.

" Know thy selfe that thou mayst fear God : know God, that thou mayst love him ; in this, thou art initiated to wisdom ; in that, perfected."—*Quarles.*

---

6. *" Come unto Me, all ye that labour and are heavy laden, and I will give you rest."*—MATTHEW xi. 28.

" None here is happy but in part ;
Full bliss is bliss divine ;
There dwells some wish in every heart,
And doubtless one in thine."—

Cowper.

" Man without religion is the creature of circumstances. Religion is above all circumstances, and will lift him up above them."—*Hare.*

2

7. "*The Spirit also helpeth our infirmities: for we know not what we should pray for as we ought: but the Spirit itself maketh intercession for us.*"—ROMANS viii. 26.

> "Prayer is the soul's sincere desire,
> Uttered or unexpressed :
> The motion of a hidden fire
> That burns within the breast."

"The sphere of our belief is much more extensive than the sphere of our knowledge."—*Sir W. Hamilton.*

8. "*The liberal soul shall be made fat.*"—PROVERBS xi. 25.

> "What though from fortune's lavish bounty
> No mighty treasures we possess,
> We'll find within our pittance plenty,
> And be content without excess."

"Never put much confidence in such as put no confidence in others. A man prone to suspect evil is mostly looking in his neighbour for what he sees in himself."—*Guesses at Truth.*

9. "*Him that cometh to Me I will in no wise cast out.*"— JOHN vi. 37.

> "What though I cannot see my king,
> Neither in person nor in coin ;
> Yet contemplation is a thing
> That renders what I have not, mine."

"Here you have that which in itself is good, made better by the store of it, and best by the welcome to it."—*Fuller.*

10. *" Blessed are they which do hunger and thirst after righteousness."—*MATTHEW v. 6.

" The thought of this bids me go on,
    And wait my dissolution
    With hope and comfort."—
                                        H. King.

" There is nothing, no, nothing, innocent or good, that dies, and
is forgotten : let us hold to that faith."—*Dickens.*

---

11. *" Call upon Me in the day of trouble : I will deliver thee."—*
PSALM l. 15.

"Who could have thought my shrivelled heart
    Could have recovered greenness ?   It was gone
Quite underground ; as flowers depart
    To see their mother-root, when they have blown."—
                                        G. Herbert.

" The joy resulting from the diffusion of blessings to all around
us, is the purest and sublimest that can ever enter the human mind,
and can be conceived only by those who have experienced it."—
Porteus.

---

12. *" They that seek the Lord shall not want any good thing."—*
PSALM xxxiv. 10.

" Still shall each kind returning season
    Sufficient for our wishes give ;
For we will live a life of reason,
    And that's the only life to live."

" Life appears to me too short to be spent in nursing animosity,
or registering wrongs."—*C. Brontë.*

4

13. "*When He, the Spirit of truth, is come, He will guide you into all truth.*"—JOHN xvi. 13.

"Oh how much more doth beauty beauteous seem
    By that sweet ornament which truth doth give !
The rose looks fair, but fairer we it deem,
    For that sweet odour which doth in it live."—
                           Shakspere.

"When truth is revealed, let custom give place ; let no man prefer custom before reason and truth."—*Augustine.*

---

14. "*Is any among you afflicted ? let him pray.*"—JAMES v. 13.

"Blest proofs of power and grace divine,
    That meet us in his word !
May every deep-felt care of mine
    Be trusted with the Lord."
                           Cowper.

"Not all the subtilties of metaphysics can make me doubt a moment of the immortality of the soul, and of a beneficent providence."—*Rousseau.*

---

15. *We have not an high priest which cannot be touched with the feeling of our infirmities.*"—HEBREWS iv. 15.

"God has enough to human kind disclosed ;
    Our fleshly garments He awhile received,
And walked as if the Godhead were deposed,
    Yet could be then but by a few believed."—
                           Davenant.

"Every man rejoices twice when he has a partner of his joy ; a friend shares my sorrow and makes it but a moiety ; but he swells my joy and makes it double."—*Taylor.*

5

16. *"O taste and see that the Lord is good: blessed is the man that trusteth in Him."*—PSALM xxxiv. 8.

> "Lord, it is my chief complaint,
>   That my love is weak and faint ;
> Yet I love thee and adore,—
>   Oh ! for grace to love thee more."

"God is the source and fountain of love, and which may be divided into three parts—the receiving from Him, the conforming to Him, and the reposing and trusting in Him."—*Burton.*

---

17. *" Jesus saith—I am the way, the truth, and the life."*—JOHN xiv. 6.

> "My soul, there is a country,
>   Afar beyond the stars,
> Where stands a winged sentry,
>   All skilful in the wars.
> There, above noise and danger,
>   Sweet Peace sits crowned with smiles,
> And One, born in a manger,
>   Commands the beauteous files."—
>
> *Vaughan.*

"How calmly may we commit ourselves to the hands of Him who bears up the world."—*Richter.*

---

18. *" Be ye all of one mind, having compassion one of another, love as brethren, be pitiful, be courteous."*—I PETER iii. 8.

> "There are no ills, but what we make
>   By giving shape and names to things ;
> Which is the dangerous mistake,
>   That causes all our sufferings."—
>
> *Cotton.*

"By love's delightful influence the attack of ill-humour is resisted, the violence of our passions abated, the bitter cup of affliction sweetened, all the injuries of the world alleviated."—*Zimmerman.*

6

19. *"If any man sin, we have an advocate with the Father Jesus Christ the righteous."*—1 JOHN ii. 1.

" My sins that pierced thy hands, thy feet,
    Thy head, thy heart, and every part of thee,
And on the cross made life and death to meet,
    Death to thyself, and life to me ;
Thy very fall does save ; O happy strife,
That struck God dead, but raisèd man to life."—

Washbourne.

" He that cannot forgive others, breaks the bridge over which he must pass himself ; for every man has need to be forgiven."—*Lord Herbert.*

20. *" There is therefore now no condemnation to them which are in Christ Jesus."*—ROMANS viii. 1.

" Death, be not proud, though some have called thee
    Mighty and dreadful, for thou art not so ;
For those, whom thou think'st thou dost overthrow,
    Die not, poor Death."—

Donne.

" It is impossible that anything so natural, so necessary, and so universal as death, should ever have been designed by Providence as an evil to mankind."—*Swift.*

21. *" God commendeth his love toward us, in that, while we were yet sinners, Christ died for us."*—ROMANS v. 8.

" O holy Hope ! and high Humility !
    High as the heavens above !
These are your walks, and you have showed them me,
    To kindle my cold love."

" Humanity is never so beautiful as when praying for forgiveness or else forgiving another."—*Richter.*

7

22. "*Watch and pray, that ye enter not into temptation: the spirit indeed is willing, but the flesh is weak.*"—MATTHEW xxvi. 41.

> "Restraining prayer, we cease to fight;
> Prayer makes the Christian's armour bright;
> And Satan trembles when he sees
> The weakest saint upon his knees."

"As there are goods in life possible to be obtained, and evils capable of being avoided, so we should provide ourselves with proper means to obtain the one, and to escape the other."—*Conybeare.*

23. "*He is able also to save them to the uttermost that come unto God by Him.*"—HEBREWS vii. 25.

> "Christ our Lord is ever near
> Those who follow Him;
> But we cannot see Him here,
> For our eyes are dim.—
> There is a most happy place,
> Where men always see his face."

"There is something in the thought of being surrounded, even upon earth, by the majesty on high, that gives a peculiar elevation and serenity of soul."—*Mathew.*

24. "*Cast thy burden upon the Lord, and He shall sustain thee.*"—PSALM lv. 22.

> "Why was I born, ye angels? was it well?
> Ye might have killed me, such a little thing!
> And I had been in Heaven all this while,
> And missed mine heritage of suffering.
> Would it have been a loss? I cannot tell;
> God knows."—
>
> *S. Williams.*

"The fortitude of a Christian consists in patience."—*Dryden.*

8

25. " *There is one God, and one mediator between God and men, the man Christ Jesus; who gave Himself a ransom for all.*"—1 TIMOTHY ii. 5, 6.

> " Be glad, the world of toils and scorns
>   But perfects him whom first it mars ;
> O, love him for his crown of thorns,
>   Then praise him for his crown of stars."—
>
> *Lynch.*

" The Christian expects his reward, not as due to merit, but as connected, in a constitution of grace, with those acts which grace enables him to perform."—*Cecil.*

---

26. " *Thou wilt keep him in perfect peace, whose mind is stayed on Thee.*"—ISAIAH xxvi. 3.

> " Think not thou canst sigh a sigh,
>   And thy Maker is not by.
>   Think not thou canst weep a tear,
>   And thy Maker is not near."—
>
> *W. Blake.*

" Peace is the proper result of the Christian temper."—*Patrick.*

---

27. " *My God, let, I beseech thee, thine eyes be open, and let thine ears be attent unto the prayer that is made in this place.*"—2 CHRONICLES vi. 40.

> " Sacred Saviour, with thy words I woo
>   Thee to forgive, and not be bitter to
>   Such as thou know'st do not know what they do."—
>
> *Charles the First.*

" In mental prayer we confess God's omniscience, in vocal prayer we call angels to witness."—*Taylor.*

28. "*God saw everything that He had made, and, behold, it was very good.*"—GENESIS i. 31.

> "The heaven it is His dwelling-place,
> The earth His little footstool low ;
> His works are all before His face,
> Of hearts the secrets He does know ;
> And everything as in a glass
> He sees before it come to pass."—
>
> *Hume.*

"We are raised by science to an understanding of the infinite wisdom and goodness which the Creator has displayed in all his works."—*Brougham.*

29. "*The spirit itself beareth witness with our spirit, that we are the children of God: and if children, then heirs ; heirs of God, and joint-heirs with Christ.*"—ROMANS viii. 16, 17.

> "Joy for the promise of our loftier homes !
> Joy for the promise of another birth !
> For oft oppressive unto pain becomes
> The riddle of the earth."—
>
> *Burbidge.*

"Our powers owe much of their energy to our hopes."—*Johnson.*

30. "*Why sleep ye ? rise and pray.*"—LUKE xxii. 46.

> "Awake my soul, stretch every nerve,
> And press with vigour on ;
> A heavenly race demands thy zeal,
> And an immortal crown."

"Life's evening, we may rest assured will take its character from the day which has preceded it."—*Shuttleworth.*

31. *"The fruit of the Spirit is love, joy, peace, long-suffering, gentleness, goodness, faith, meekness, temperance: against such there is no law."*—GALATIANS V. 22, 23.

> " Sweet order hath its draught of bliss
> Graced with the pearl of God's consent,
> Ten times ecstatic in that 'tis
> Considerate and innocent."—

Patmore.

" As for that wife of mine, when she sets forth the maternal plea, and appeals to the exuberant school of philosophers, I know there is no reasoning with her. I leave her to kiss out the rest of the argument over the children."—*Thackeray.*

FEBRUARY.

1. "*In all their affliction He was afflicted, and the angel of His presence saved them.*"—ISAIAH lxiii. 9.

" O ye who serve, remember One
    The worker's way who trod ;
He served as man, but now his throne,
    It is the throne of God :
The sceptre He hath to us shown
    Is like a blossoming rod."—

Lynch.

" All powerful souls have kindred with each other."—*Coleridge.*

---

2. "*My times are in Thy hand.*"—PSALM xxxi. 15.

" Thou wilt not leave us in the dust :
    Thou madest man, he knows not why ;
    He thinks he was not made to die ;
And thou hast made him : thou art just."—

Tennyson.

" Nor in all these things can I find any safe place for my soul, but only in Thyself ; there may my scattered members be gathered, so that nothing of me shall be separated from Thee."—*St. Augustine.*

---

3. "*I know that my Redeemer liveth.*"—JOB xix. 25.

" Never then be scorning
    Heaven's cloudless morning,
Brighter worlds are dawning :
    Be grateful, be faithful ;
    Christ lives for thee."—

Hodder.

" The path of the sinner back to God is brighter and brighter all the way up to the smile of the face and the touch of the hand ; and *that* is salvation."—*Beecher.*

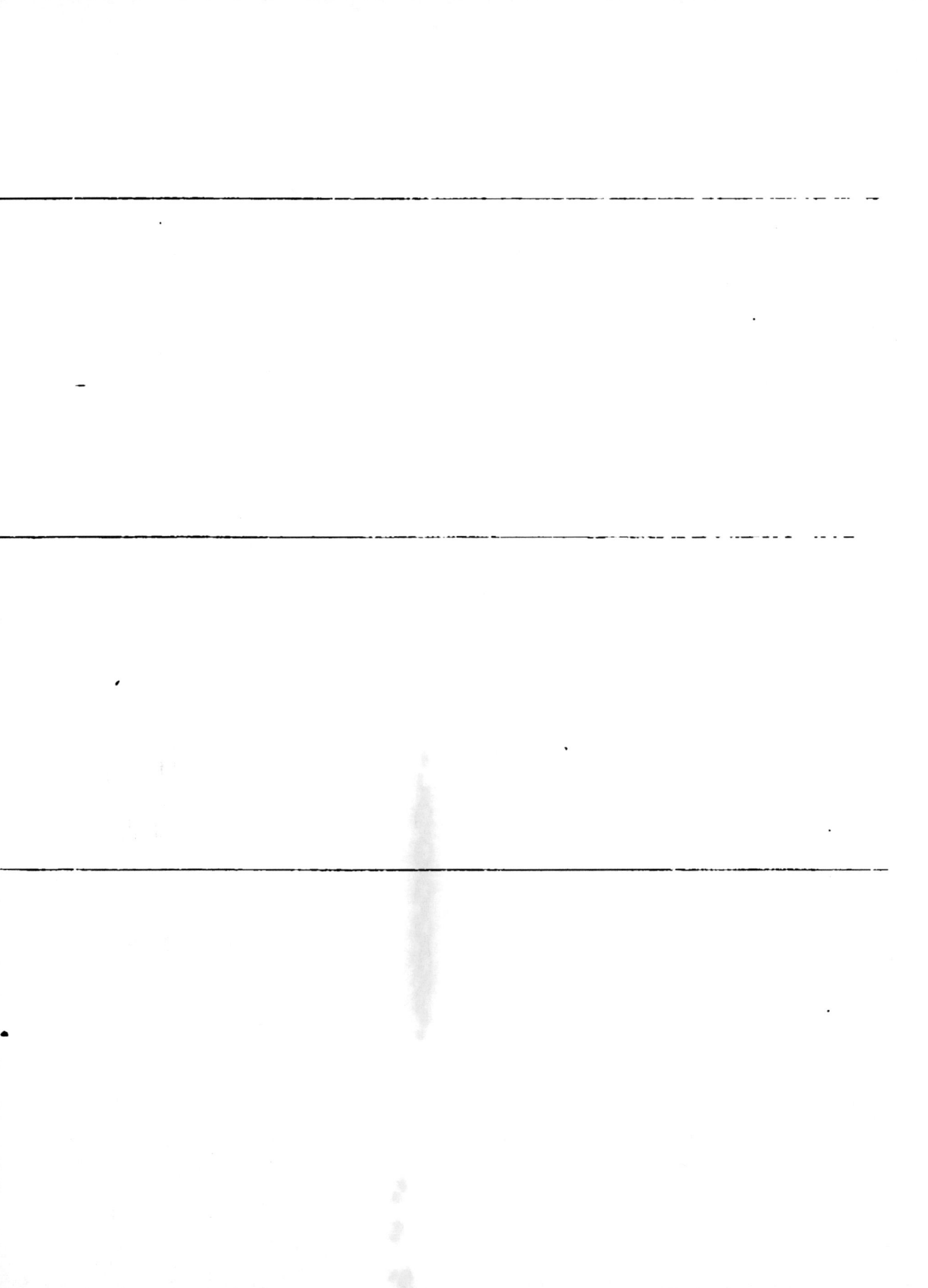

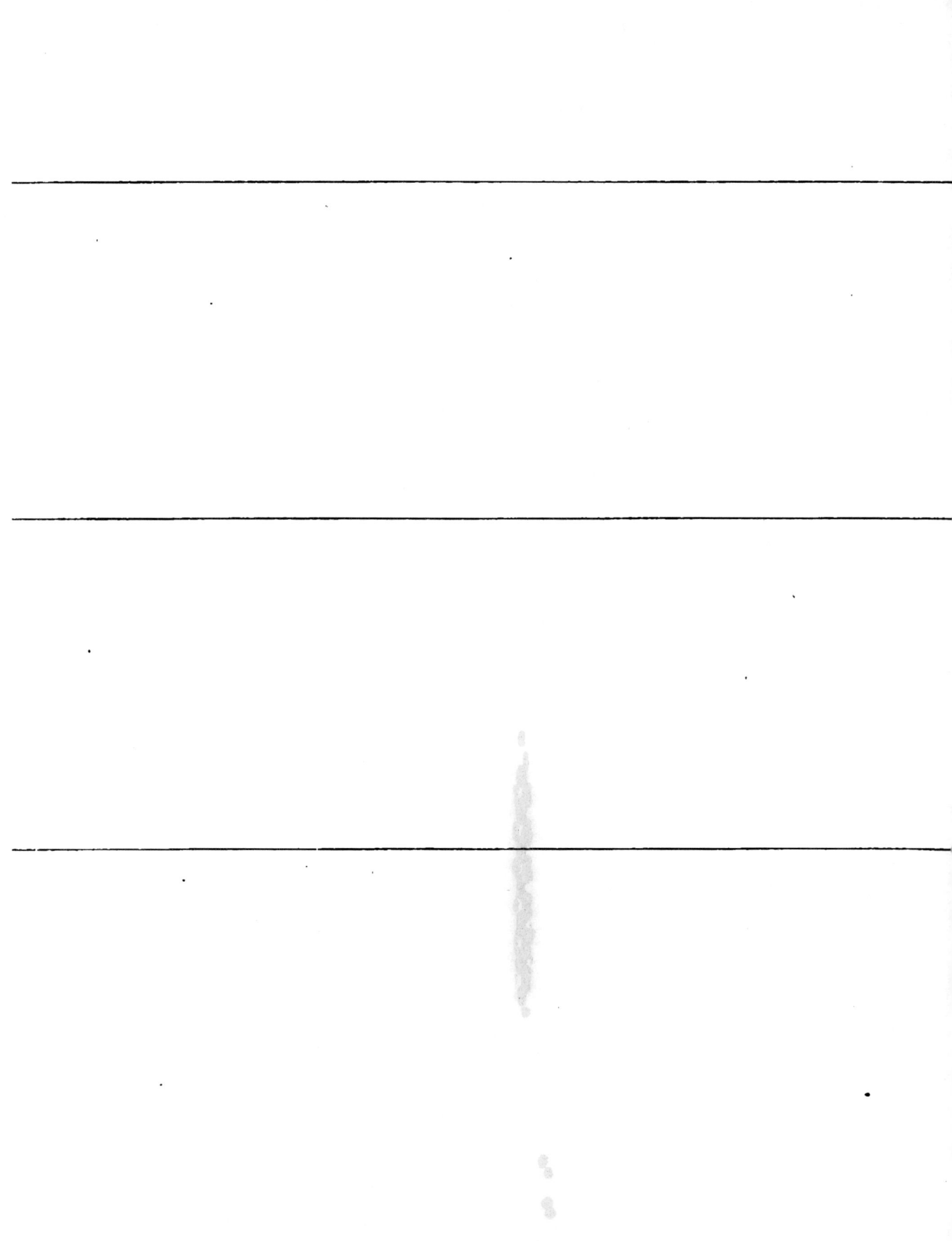

4. "*I will greatly rejoice in the Lord, my soul shall be joyful in my God.*"—ISAIAH lxi. 10.

"Let the voice of all creation,
Earth and heaven's triumphant host,
Praise the God of our salvation,
Father, Son, and Holy Ghost."

"Researches into the springs of natural bodies and their motions, should awaken us to admiration at the wondrous wisdom of our Creator."—*Watts.*

5. "*Love is strong as death; jealousy is cruel as the grave.*"—SOLOMON'S SONG viii. 6.

"Foul jealousy! thou turnest love divine
To joyless dread, and mak'st the loving heart
With hateful thoughts to languish and to pine,
And feed itself with self-consuming smart;
Of all the passions in the mind, thou vilest art."—

Spenser.

"No man is greatly jealous, who is not in some measure guilty."
—*Whichcote.*

6. "*Heaviness in the heart of man maketh it stoop: but a good word maketh it glad.*"—PROVERBS xii. 25.

"While life's dark maze I tread,
And griefs around me spread,
Be Thou my Guide;
Bid darkness turn to day,
Wipe sorrow's tears away,
Nor let me ever stray
From Thee aside."

"Good words are worth much and cost little."—*Herbert.*

13

7. "*God giveth to a man that is good in His sight wisdom, and knowledge, and joy.*"—ECCLESIASTES ii. 26.

"Is it well to be clever? you question, my
daughter.   I know not;
I have never been clever myself, only
patient, and faithful,—
Giving out, as a lamp might, the light
that was kindled within me;
Neither kindling nor radiance mine
own, only mine was the burning."—
Williams.

"Most certainly that superior wisdom which corrects, reproves and informs a man against his own inclinations, can be no part of himself."—*Fénelon.*

---

8. "*Let your light so shine before men, that they may see yonr good works, and glorify your Father which is in heaven.*"—MATTHEW v. 16.

"And every virtue we possess,
And every conquest won,
And every thought of holiness,
Are His alone."

"No man is so insignificant as to be sure his example can do no hurt."—*Clarendon.*

---

9. "*He talked with them, and saith unto them, Be of good cheer: it is I; be not afraid.*"—MARK vi. 50.

"God is our sun and shield,
Our light and our defence;
With gifts his hands are filled,
We draw our blessings thence."

"I have a power in my soul which enables me to perceive God: I am as certain as that I live that nothing is so near to me as God."—*Tauler.*

14

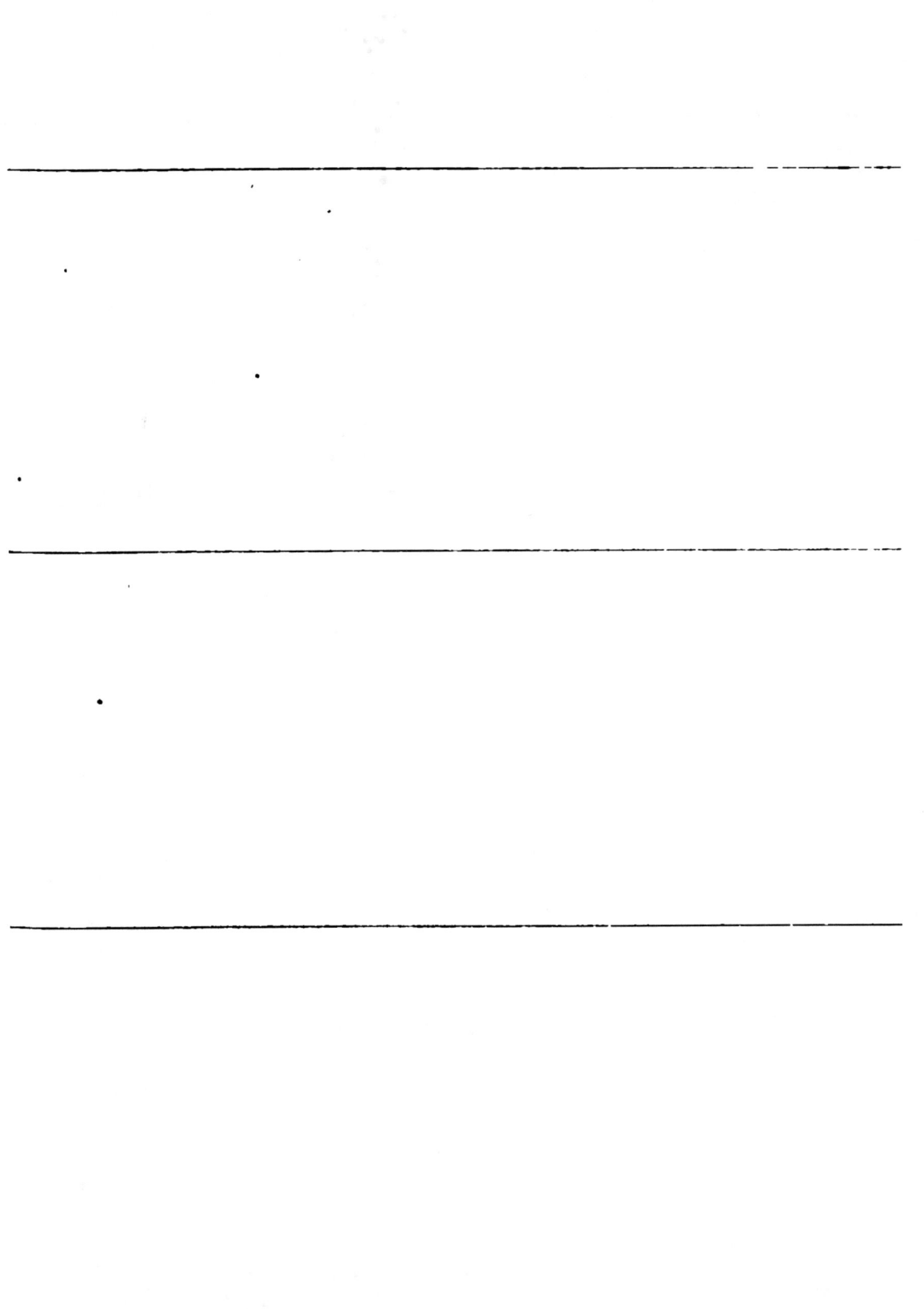

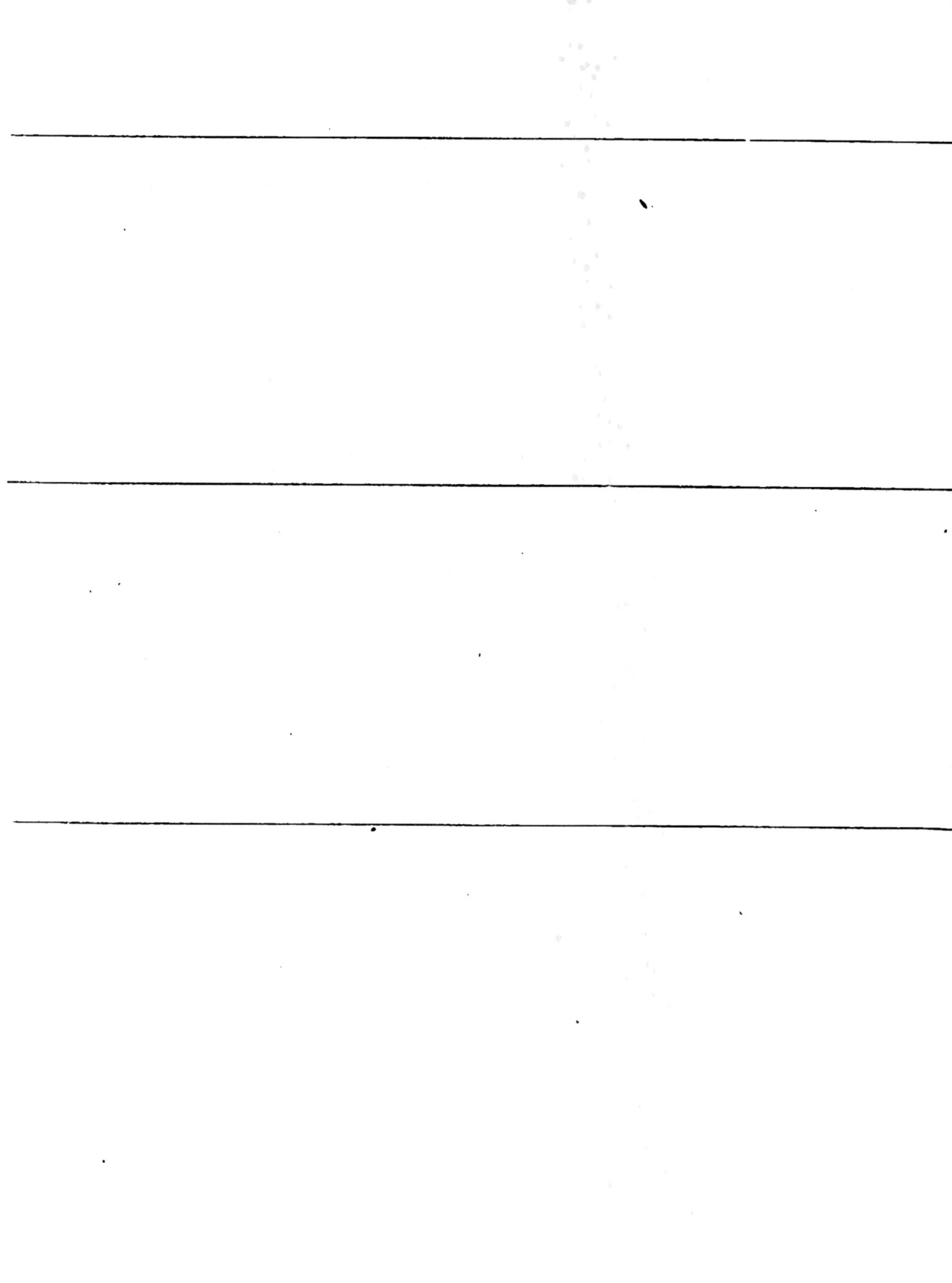

10. "*Grace to you and peace from God our Father, and the Lord Jesus Christ.*"—ROMANS i. 7.

"Come, gracious Spirit, heavenly Dove,
With light and comfort from above :
Be thou our Guardian, thou our Guide ;
O'er every thought and step preside."

"What is being religious, but always seeing God's infinite love in everything, and loving Him all the time ?"—*Clarke.*

---

11. "*In everything ye are enriched by Him, in all utterance, and in all knowledge.*"—I CORINTHIANS i. 5

"Lord, how thy wonders are displayed
Where'er I turn mine eye !
If I survey the ground I tread,
Or gaze upon the sky."

"Good-nature, by which I mean beneficence and candour, is the product of right reason, which of necessity will give allowance to the feelings of others, by considering that there is nothing perfect in mankind."—*Dryden.*

---

12. "*Blessed be God, even the Father of our Lord Jesus Christ, the Father of mercies, and the God of all comfort.*"—2 CORINTHIANS i. 3.

"Lord, when in silent hours I muse
Upon myself and Thee,
I seem to hear the stream of Life
That runs invisibly."—
Lynch.

"He offers pardon to the guilty, purity to the defiled, peace, joy, hope, heaven to the wretched, or that which includes them all—that strange unearthly blessing—*rest*, to the weary and heavy-laden soul."—*Dr. Caird.*

13. "*The life which I now live in the flesh I live by the faith of the Son of God, who loved me, and gave Himself for me.*"—GALATIANS ii. 20.

"God only knows the love of God."

"It makes the wounded spirit whole,
And calms the troubled breast;
'Tis manna to the hungry soul,
And to the weary, rest."

"Notwithstanding all that thou hast learned of Him, remember thou hast but read the child's first primer; thou art as yet on one of the lower forms."—*Spurgeon.*

---

14. "*What shall a man give in exchange for his soul?*"—MARK viii. 37.

"I'll sit me down, no more beguiled
By those who are too serpent-wise;
And seek my Saviour through the eyes
And pure heart of a little child."—

G. Massey.

"Attend carefully to these words."—*Krummacher.*

---

15. "*By grace are ye saved through faith; and that not of yourselves: it is the gift of God.*"—EPHESIANS ii. 8.

"In a garden man became
Heir of sin, and death, and shame;
Jesus, in a garden wins
Life, and pardon for our sins;
Through his hour of agony
Praying in Gethsemane."

"Jesus teaches us to know God by showing Him to us as our Father and Friend."—*Clarke.*

16. "*A man shall be commended according to his wisdom.*"—
PROVERBS xii. 8.

"Who loves not knowledge ? who shall rail
    Against her beauty ? may she mix
    With men and prosper ! who shall fix
Her pillars? Let her work prevail."—

Tennyson.

"The first point of wisdom is to discern that which is false ; the second, to know that which is true."

---

17. "*As the earth bringeth forth her bud, and as the garden causeth the things that are sown in it to spring forth; so the Lord God will cause righteousness and praise to spring forth before all the nations.*"—ISAIAH lxi. 11.

"All nature has a voice,
    All nature can rejoice ;
    And every lesson heard
    Is God's unwritten word,
Which speaks around, below, above,
And ever tells us, ' God is Love.' "—

Hodder.

"The greatest truths are the simplest : and so are the greatest men."—*Hare.*

---

18. "*Let your moderation be known unto all men.*"—PHILIPPIANS
iv. 5.

"Jesus, great friend of open speech
    Which wisdom prompts and wisdom leads
True courage give, discretion teach,
    To every one for thee who pleads."—

Lynch.

"Moderation—this is the centre wherein all both divine and human philosophy meet."—*Hall.*

19. "*Better is a poor and a wise child than an old and foolish king who will no more be admonished.*"—ECCLESIASTES iv. 13.

"The wise man, says the Bible, walks with God,
　Surveys far on the endless line of life ;
Values his soul, thinks of eternity ;
　Both worlds considers, and provides for both."—
　　　　　　　　　　　　　　　　Pollok.

"Wisdom teaches us to do, as well as to talk ; and to make our words and actions all of a colour."—*Seneca.*

---

20. "*Blessed are the pure in heart : for they shall see God.*"—MATTHEW v. 8.

"If thou art my shield and my sun,
　The night is no darkness to me ;
And, fast as my moments roll on,
　They bring me but closer to thee."

"Deride not him whom the looser world calls Puritane, lest thou offend a little one : if he be an hypocrite, God, that knowes him, will reward him ; if zealous, God, that loves him, will revenge him."
—*Quarles.*

---

21. "*We are sure that the judgment of God is according to truth.*"
—ROMANS ii. 2.

"Holy, Holy, Holy ! though the darkness hide thee,
　Though the eye of sinful man thy glory may not see ;
Only thou art holy : there is none beside thee,
　Perfect in power, in love, and purity."

"There is nothing that God has judged good for us that He has not given us the means to accomplish, both in the natural and moral world."—*Burke.*

22. *"When it goeth well with the righteous, the city rejoiceth."*
PROVERBS xi. 10.

"Still in the paths of honour persevere,
And not, from past or present ills, despair;
For blessings ever wait on virtuous deeds,
And though a late, a sure reward succeeds."—
Congreve.

"Let honour be to us as strong an obligation as necessity is to others."—*Pliny.*

---

23. *"God is faithful."*—1 CORINTHIANS i. 9.

"Earthly friends may fail or leave us,
One day soothe, the next day grieve us,
But this friend will ne'er deceive us.
O how He loves!"

"I should prefer a firm religious faith to every other blessing; for it makes life a discipline of goodness; creates new hopes, when all earthly hopes vanish; and throws over the decay, the destruction, of existence, the most gorgeous of all lights."—*Sir H. Davy.*

---

24. *"Thou shalt also be a crown of glory in the hand of the Lord, and a royal diadem in the hand of thy God."*—ISAIAH lxii. 3.

"Leave God to order all thy ways,
And hope in Him whate'er betide;
Thou'lt find Him in the evil days
Thy all-sufficient strength and guide.
Who trusts in God's unchanging love
Builds on the rock that nought can move."—
Newmarch.

"Never yet did there exist a full faith in the Divine Word which did not expand the intellect while it purified the heart."—*Coleridge.*

25. *"Our rejoicing is this, the testimony of our conscience."*— 2 CORINTHIANS i. 12.

"What stronger breastplate than a heart untainted ?
Thrice is he armed that hath his quarrel just ;
And he but naked, though locked up in steel,
Whose conscience with injustice is corrupted."—

Shakspere.

"There is, then, in our heart of hearts, an innate principle of justice and of virtue upon which we judge our own actions and those of others ; and it is to this principle that we give the name of Conscience."—*Rousseau.*

---

26. *"Because ye are sons, God hath sent forth the spirit of His Son into your hearts, crying, Abba, Father."*—GALATIANS iv. 6.

"His wisdom is sublime,
His heart profoundly kind ;
God never is before his time,
And never is behind."—

Lynch.

"Holiness supposes nothing unsocial, withdraws no one from those living sympathies that gladden human life. On the contrary it quickens all the most gentle and loving affinities."—*Bushnell.*

---

27. *"Blessed are the peacemakers: for they shall be called the children of God."*—MATTHEW v. 9.

"O beauteous Peace,
Sweet union of a state ! what else but thou
Gives safety, strength, and glory to a people ?"—

Thompson.

"Blessed is the man whom eternal truth teacheth, not by obscure figures and transient sounds, but by direct and full communication."—*Thomas à Kempis.*

---

28. "*Salt is good; but if the salt have lost his saltness, wherewith will ye season it? Have salt in yourselves, and have peace one with another.*"—MARK ix. 50.

> "Work thou in me, and heavenward guide
> My thoughts and wishes, that my heart
> Waver no more, nor turn aside,
> But fix for ever where thou art."

"One of the saddest things about human nature is, that a man may guide others in the path of life without walking in it himself; that he may be a pilot, and yet a castaway."—*Hare.*

---

29. "*Better is an handful with quietness, than both the hands full with travail and vexation of spirit.*"—ECCLESIASTES iv. 6.

> "I feel no care of coin ;
> Well-doing is my wealth :
> My mind to me an empire is,
> While grace affordeth health."—
> > *Southwell.*

"That man is not poor who has the use of things necessary."—*Horace.*

---

1. "*O Lord, Thou art our father; we are the clay, and Thou our potter; and we all are the work of Thy hand.*"—ISAIAH lxiv. 8.

> " Our little systems have their day ;
>> They have their day and cease to be :
>> They are but broken lights of Thee,
> And Thou, O Lord, art more than they."—
>>>>> *Tennyson.*

" The delight is inexpressible of being able to follow the marvellous works of the Great Author of Nature, and to trace the unbounded power and exquisite skill which are exhibited by the most minute, as well as the mightiest, parts of His system."—*Brougham.*

---

2. " *Our Father which art in heaven, Hallowed be Thy name.*"—MATTHEW vi. 9.

> " Let the incense of your best endeavours
>> Unto God ascend,
> 'Till He come to close the diapason,
>> And to preach the end."—
>>>> *A. Horton.*

" Without prayer there is no such thing as Religion ; all that is so called will melt into nothingness if it be not crystallized into Prayer."—*Palmer.*

---

3. " *Jesus said—Suffer the little children to come unto Me, and forbid them not: for of such is the kingdom of heaven.*" MARK x. 14.

> " Let children come ;
>> Love has made all ready ;
> Our Father's arms,
>> How strong they are, how steady !"—*Lynch.*

" Oh ! how precious to me have been the prattlings of little children, and those subtle questions and those still subtler replies that I have heard coming from their spotless lips, and have listened to as to oracular breathings !"—*Gilfillan.*

4. *" There is no respect of persons with God."*—ROMANS ii. 11.

" Can we, whose souls are lighted with wisdom from on high,
Can we to lands benighted the lamp of life deny?
Salvation! oh, salvation! the joyful sound proclaim,
Till earth's remotest nation has learn'd Messiah's name."—
Heber.

" Religion presents few difficulties to the humble, many to the proud, insuperable ones to the vain."—*Hare.*

5. *" The merciful man doeth good to his own soul."*—PROVERBS xi. 17.

" The quality of mercy is not strained;
It droppeth as the gentle rain from heaven
Upon the place beneath: it is twice bless'd:
It blesseth him that gives, and him that takes:
'Tis mightiest in the mightiest."—
Shakspere.

" In the intercourse of social life, it is by little acts of watchful kindness—it is by words, by tones, by gestures, by looks, that affection is won and preserved."—*Sala.*

6. *" Keep thy foot when thou goest to the house of God, and be more ready to hear, than to give the sacrifice of fools."*—ECCLESIASTES v. i.

" Let knowledge grow from more to more.
But more of reverence in us dwell;
That mind and soul, according well,
May make one music."—
Tennyson.

" Give not thy tongue too great a liberty, lest it take thee prisoner."
—*Quarles.*

7. "*Eye hath not seen, nor ear heard, neither have entered into the heart of man, the things which God hath prepared for them that love Him.*"—1 CORINTHIANS ii. 9.

> "Let us with a gladsome mind
> Praise the Lord, for He is kind ;
> For his mercies aye endure,
> Ever faithful, ever sure."

"The elect are whosoever will, and the non-elect whosoever won't."—*H. W. Beecher.*

8. "*If ye be willing and obedient, ye shall eat the good of the land.*"—ISAIAH i. 19.

> "High as the heavens are raised
> Above the ground we tread,
> So far the riches of his grace
> Our highest thoughts exceed."

"To obey God is perfect liberty : he that does this shall be free, safe, and quiet ; all his actions shall succeed to his wishes."—*Seneca.*

9. "*I beseech you that ye would confirm your love toward Him.*"
2 CORINTHIANS ii. 8.

> "Jesus calls us—from the worship
> Of the vain world's golden store,
> From each idol that would keep us—
> Saying, Christian, love me more."

"Love is such an affection as cannot so properly be said to be in the soul, as the soul to be in that."—*South.*

10. *" Whatsoever ye would that men should do to you, do ye even so to them."*—MATTHEW vii. 12.

" And no work is e'er too humble,
For the roughest path e'er known
Will our Saviour travel with us,
If we look to Him alone."

" The great duty of life is not to give pain ; and the most acute reasoner cannot find an excuse for one who voluntarily wounds the heart of a fellow-creature."—*Bremer.*

11. *" It is good to be zealously affected always in a good thing."*— GALATIANS iv. 18.

" Be thou ardent, then, and gentle :
Ardent, for the cause is great ;
Gentle, lest thou wound unthinking,
And repent too late."

"Zeal for the public good is the characteristic of a man of honour and a gentleman."—*Steele.*

12. *" Let all bitterness, and wrath, and anger, and clamour, and evil speaking, be put away from you."*—EPHESIANS iv. 31.

" From evil men whose tongues are swords,
Who speak and have not understood,
Lord, keep us !   From the strife of words,
Fold up our hearts in something good."—
G. Macdonald.

" Moral evils are of your own making ; and undoubtedly the greater part of them may be prevented."—*Southey.*

13. *"A good man leaveth an inheritance to his children's children."*—
PROVERBS xiii. 22.

" For He, the merciful and true,
　Hath saved His people hitherto ;
　Not willing that the soul should die
　Though great its past iniquity."

" There is nothing which children imitate, or apply more readily,
than expressions of affection and aversion, of approbation, hatred,
resentment, and the like."—*Paley.*

---

14. *" Where the Spirit of the Lord is, there is liberty."*—
2 CORINTHIANS iii. 17.

" How blessed, in the wearing strife,
　Amid strongholds undone,
　So to be taught that Light and Life—
　That Light and Love are one !"—

Waring.

" I know not what should more cheer and gladden a Christian than
to see his spiritual life losing everything of an exotic character ; to
have it set in the open air, welcoming the wind from every quarter."—
Author of *Patience of Hope.*

---

15. *" What if some did not believe ? shall their unbelief make the
faith of God without effect ?"*—ROMANS iii. 3.

" God's hand is on the plough.—So be thou still.—
　Thou canst not see Him, for thine eyes are dim ;
　But wait in patience, put thy trust in Him—
　Give thanks for love, and leave thee to His will."

" The infinite is more sure than any other fact."—*Carlyle.*

26

16. "*Be not rash with thy mouth, and let not thine heart be hasty to utter anything before God: for God is in heaven, and thou upon earth: therefore let thy words be few.*"—ECCLESIASTES v. 2

"Trust me, the worth of words is such
  They guard all noble things,
And that this rash irreverent touch
  Has jarred some golden strings."—
                          A. A. Proctor.

"Words are the counters of wise men, and the money of fools."—*Hobbes.*

---

17. "*Lord, if Thou wilt, Thou canst make me clean.*"—MATTHEW viii. 2.

"We would put on Thy likeness—we, the least
  And most unworthy. Ay, each piercing thorn,
  In thy name patiently and meekly worn,
Shall bear a blossom for the bridal feast."—
                          A. Cambridge.

"If thy sin trouble thee, let that trouble comfort thee; as pleasure in the remembrance of sin exasperates justice, so sorrow in the repentance of sin mollifies mercy."—*Quarles.*

---

18. "*With God all things are possible.*"—MARK x. 27.

"Faith can never know the free salvation
  Which Jesus for his people will prepare:
Then will I wait in peaceful expectation
  Till the Good Shepherd come to take me there:
Enough for me is this—a blissful end I see,
Though now I know not what I yet shall be."

"God never does things by halves.—He never leaves any work unfinished."—*Hare.*

27

19. *"Jerusalem which is above is free."*—GALATIANS iv. 26.

"Brief life is here our portion ; brief sorrow, short-lived care ;
The life that knows no ending, the tearless life, is there.—
O happy retribution : short toil, eternal rest :
For mortals and for sinners a mansion with the bless'd."

"Every promise is built upon four pillars :—God's justice or holiness, which will not suffer Him to deceive ; His grace or goodness, which will not suffer Him to forget ; His truth, which will not suffer Him to change ; and His power, which makes Him able to accomplish."—*Salter.*

20. *"He that is soon angry dealeth foolishly."*—PROVERBS xiv. 17.

"Oh ! let me then at length be taught
What I am still so slow to learn ;
That God is Love, and changes not,
Nor knows the shadow of a turn."

"When anger rises, think of the consequences."—*Confucius.*

21. *"We are labourers together with God : ye are God's husbandry, ye are God's building."*—I CORINTHIANS iii. 9.

"Thy stream of outward comforts came
From Him who built this earthly frame ;
Whate'er I want his bounty gives,
By whom my soul for ever lives."

"O God, who art the truth, make me one with Thee in everlasting love ! I am often weary of reading, and weary of hearing ; in Thee alone is the sum of my desire !"—*Thomas à Kempis.*

22. "*In everything by prayer and supplication with thanksgiving let your requests be made known unto God.*"—PHILIPPIANS iv. 6.

> " To tell the Saviour all my wants,
>   How pleasing is the task !
> Nor less to praise Him when He grants
>   Beyond what I can ask."

" Prayer opens to us, as it were, the portals of the spirit-world, in which we also have some right of citizenship.—We draw nearer to the Deity, and feel that we belong to Him."—*Zschokke.*

---

23. "*Tribulation worketh patience; and patience, experience; and experience, hope.*"—ROMANS v. 3, 4.

> " Then the sorrow of life made my righteousness softer,
>   more tender ;
> And I painted the flowers by the wayside, and knelt as I
>   painted ;
> And men said, ' He is growing, this painter,—is nearing
>   the great.' "—
>
> *Sadie.*

" The text, whether of prophet or poet, expands for whatever we can put into it."—*G. Eliot.*

---

24. "*Whatsoever ye do, do it heartily, as to the Lord, and not unto men.*"—COLOSSIANS iii. 23.

> " Lord, through the spirit whom Thy Son
> Hath bidden us in prayer to ask,
> Arm us with might that every task,
> Whate'er we do, in Thee be done."

" When thy hand hath done a good act, ask thy heart whether it was well done."—*Fuller.*

25. "*Let us, who are of the day, be sober, putting on the breast-plate of faith and love; and for an helmet, the hope of salvation.*"—1 THESSALONIANS v. 8.

  "The purposes of life misunderstood,
    Baffle and wound us, but God only would
    That we should heed his simple words, 'Be Good.'"

"The things for which I hold life valuable, are, the satisfactions which accrue from the improvement of knowledge and the exercise of piety."—*Boyle.*

26. "*Jesus saith, I will come and heal him.—The Centurion answered, Lord, speak the word only, and my servant shall be healed.—And his servant was healed in the selfsame hour.*"—MATTHEW viii. 7, 8, 13.

  "And Thou art near us in our bliss,
    And near in all our woe ;
    Our strength for toil and conflict this,
    Our shield from every foe."—
                              Downton.

"To know that there are some souls, hearts and minds, here and there, who trust us, and whom we trust ; some on whom we can always rely, and who will always rely on us, makes a paradise of this great world."—*Clarke.*

27. "*The eyes of the Lord are in every place, beholding the evil and the good.*"—PROVERBS xv. 3.

  "God moves in a mysterious way,
    His wonders to perform ;
    He plants His footsteps in the sea,
    And rides upon the storm."—
                              Cowper.

"The Divine eye is always upon us, and when we least think it ; is noting all, and, whatever we may think of it, will remember all."—*De Vere.*

28. "*Suffer not thy mouth to cause thy flesh to sin; neither say thou before the angel, that it was an error.*"—ECCLESIASTES v. 6.

> "Watch, my soul, and pray;
> Put thee in array;
> For the tempter's snares are nearest
> When the danger least thou fearest:
> Such is Satan's way;
> Watch, my soul, and pray."—
>
> *Tait.*

"Certainly the mistakes that we male and female mortals make when we have our own way might fairly raise some wonder that we are so fond of it."—*G. Eliot.*

29. "*Jesus said—What would ye that I should do for you?*"—MARK x. 36.

> "Holy Father, those Thy servants
> Who did bring the good news here
> Said that Thou wast ever with them,
> That they knew not how to fear;
> Art Thou with us, too, O Father?
> Suffer us to feel Thee near."—
>
> *Williams.*

"God is pleased with no music below so much as in the thanksgiving songs of relieved widows, of supported orphans, of rejoicing, and comforted, and thankful persons."—*Jeremy Taylor.*

30. "*What fruit had ye then in those things whereof ye are now ashamed?*"—ROMANS vi. 21.

> "The soul, a dreary province once
> Of Satan's dark domain,
> Feels a new empire formed within,
> And owns a heavenly reign."

"True repentance is to cease from sin."—*Ambrose.*

31. *"The blind man said unto Him, Lord, that I might receive my sight."*—MARK x. 51.

"Ah! brother, sister, in life's crowded street,
What bitter need there is that you and I
Should fall in love and sorrow at those feet,
And lift once more our supplicating cry!"—

Brodrick.

"Light, once kindled, spreads till all is luminous."—*Carlyle.*

1. " *There is nothing covered that shall not be revealed; and hid that shall not be known.*"—MATTHEW x. 26.

" Each thought and deed His piercing eyes
  With strictest search survey ;
The deepest shades no more disguise
  Than the full blaze of day."—

C. Wesley.

" It is a poor philosophy and a narrow religion which does not recognise God as all in all. Every moment of our lives we breathe, stand, or move in the temple of the Most High ; for the whole universe is his temple."—*Francis.*

2. " *Whosoever shall call upon the name of the Lord shall be saved.*"—ROMANS x. 13.

" Give to the winds thy fears;
  Hope, and be undismayed ;
God hears thy sighs, and counts thy tears,
  God shall lift up thy head."—

Gerhardt.

" God is ever ready, but we are very unready."—*Tauler.*

3. " *Now faith is the substance of things hoped for, the evidence of things not seen.*"—HEBREWS xi. 1.

" Is it not by far the hardest—
  Though the safest and the best—
To fulfil our common duties,
  Trusting God for all the rest ?"

" Thy ministers can pronounce the words, but cannot impart the spirit.—They administer the letter, but Thou openest the sense ; they utter the mystery, but Thou revealest its meaning."—*À Kempis.*

4. *" Let us not be weary in well doing; for in due season we shall reap, if we faint not."* —GALATIANS vi. 9

" But only wait awhile,
Until thy sun return ;
Then, lighted by that gladsome smile,
Thy heart again shall burn."—

Horton.

" God hath suited every creature He hath made with a convenient good, to which it tends, and in the obtainment of which it rests and is satisfied."—*Coleridge.*

5. *" Let not the foot of pride come against me, and let not the hand of the wicked remove me."*—PSALM xxxvi. 11.

" He that is down needs fear no fall ;
He that is low, no pride ;
He that is humble ever shall
Have God to be his guide."—

Bunyan.

" Pride either finds a desert or makes one."—*Colton.*

6. *" Behold, God exalteth by his power : who teacheth like Him ?"* —JOB xxxvi. 22.

" Our own narrow thought forsaking,—
Turning from our visions dim,—
Let us, at his voice awaking,
Learn the thoughts of God from Him."

" Only let there be God within us, and then everything outside us will become a godlike help."—*Euthanasy.*

7. *" Withhold not good from them to whom it is due, when it is in the power of thine hand to do it."*—PROVERBS iii. 27.

> " To sojourn in the world, and yet apart ;
>   To dwell with God, and still with man to feel ;
> To bear about for ever in the heart
>   The gladness which His Spirit doth reveal."

> " The truly generous is the truly wise."—*Home.*

8. *" Take my yoke upon you, and learn of Me ; for I am meek and lowly in heart : and ye shall find rest unto your souls."*—MATTHEW xi. 29.

> " Lord, I am thine, all glory to thy name ;
>   I to thy law my life, myself, resign :
> Of right Thou dost my love, my worship claim,
>   And I am thine !"

" Christ is an amply sufficient way. All may get to heaven by the same way, and none need be excluded. On it there is room, and plenty of room, for all that will."—*Dr. Cumming.*

9. *" Let love be without dissimulation."*—ROMANS xii. 9.

> " Come, thou Spirit of pure love,
>   Who dost forth from God proceed,
> Never from my heart remove,
>   Let me all thy impulse heed."—
>
>   *Lange.*

" There is but One in whom such an image of high love has appeared to us in its entire purity, and it is only by faith in Him that such self-sacrificing love is produced."—*Tholuck.*

10. *"In the day of prosperity be joyful, but in the day of adversity consider: God also hath set the one over against the other."*—ECCLESIASTES vii. 14.

> "There are briars besetting every path,
> Which call for patient care;
> There is a cross in every lot,
> And an earnest need for prayer:
> But a lowly heart that leans on Thee,
> Is happy anywhere."

"We cannot advance uninterruptedly in our spiritual, any more than in our bodily life, from one degree of brightness to another."—*Hare.*

11. *"He that spared not his own Son, but delivered Him up for us all, how shall He not with Him also freely give us all things?"*—ROMANS viii. 32.

> "Lord, if I dip my cup into the sea
> It rises full.—Such cup each soul may be,
> Such ocean is thy good!"

"Generosity, when once she is set forward, knows not how to stop, and the more familiar we are with the lovely form, the more enamoured we become of her charms."—*Pliny.*

12. *"Stand fast . . in the liberty wherewith Christ hath made us free."*—GALATIANS v. 1.

> "Patience, Lord, is all I ask,
> Only give me rest in Thee!
> Here is strength for every task,
> This the life of liberty."

"Give me the liberty to know, to think, to believe, and to utter freely, according to conscience, above all other liberties."—*Milton.*

13. *" The fear of the Lord is the beginning of knowledge."*—
PROVERBS i. 7.

" O Thou, the primal Fount of life and peace,
    Who shedd'st thy breathing quiet all around,
In me command that pain and conflict cease,
    And turn to music every jarring sound."—
Sterling.

" Every created thing glorifies God in its place, by fulfilling his
will, and the great purpose of his providence."—*Kirby.*

14. *" The word of God is quick, and powerful . . and is a discerner
of the thoughts and intents of the heart."*—HEBREWS iv. 12.

" Lord, Thou hast formed mine every part,
    Mine inmost thought is known to Thee ;
Each word, each feeling of my heart,
    Thine ear doth hear, thine eye doth see."—
R. A. Scott.

" There *is* such an Eye, though the business and struggles of the
world too often prevent us from considering this awful truth."—
De Vere.

15. *" Is anything too hard for the Lord ?"*—GENESIS xviii. 14.

" But who can speak thy wondrous deeds ?
    Thy greatness all our thoughts exceeds ;
Vast and unsearchable thy ways,
Vast and immortal be thy praise."—
Watts.

" Power is that glorious attribute of God Almighty which
furnishes the rest of his perfections."—*Collier.*

16. *"First cast out the beam out of thine own eye; and then shalt thou see clearly to cast out the mote out of thy brother's eye."*—MATTHEW vii. 5.

> "Teach me thy love to know,
>   That this new light which now I see
> May both the work and workman show—
>   Then by a sunbeam I will climb to Thee."—
>
>   *G. Herbert.*

"When thou hast profited so much that thou respectest even thyself, thou mayest let go thy tutor."—*Seneca.*

17. *"Blessed is he that considereth the poor: the Lord will deliver him in time of trouble."*—PSALM xli. 1.

> "Spirit of mercy! bow thine head,
>   Thy pinions light stretch forth,
> Descending from thy native skies,
>   Come, visit me on earth."

"Our humanity were a poor thing but for the divinity that stirs within us."—*Bacon.*

18. *"We know that all things work together for good to them that love God."*—ROMANS viii. 28.

> "Help me, my God and King,
>   Rightly thy praise to sing,
>   And Thee for everything
>   Ever adore."

"Unto them that love Him, God causeth all things to work for the best. So that with Him, by the heavenly light of steadfast faith, they see life even in death."—*Coverdale.*

19. *"Let us not be desirous of vain glory, provoking one another, envying one another."*—GALATIANS v. 26.

" Lord, rid me of this natural waywardness,
  Unworthy one who is a child of thine ;
Calm let me be when rudest winds distress,
  Nor lose occasion if the day be fine ;
But faithful to the light of sacred reason,
One heart be mine in every changing season."—

Lynch.

" He who considers himself a paragon of wisdom is sure to commit some superlatively stupid act.   That is the course of nature."— *Tieck.*

20. *" I will say unto God, Do not condemn me; show me where- fore Thou contendest with me."*—JOB x. 2.

" Thou knowest all that I would say
  Of my mistaken deeds :
Thou, in the garden of my soul,
  Know'st how to deal with weeds."—

Powers.

" God oftentimes, in the same man, distinguishes between the sinner and the creature ; as a creature, He can love him, while as a sinner He does afflict him."—*South.*

21. *" Though He were a Son, yet learned He obedience by the things which He suffered."*—HEBREWS v. 8.

" Our Master all the work hath done
  He asks of us to-day ;
Sharing his service, every one
  Share too his sonship may,
Lord, I would serve, and be a son ;
  Dismiss me not, I pray."

" Obedience is the mother of success, bringing safety."—*Æschylus.*

22. "*The Lord giveth wisdom: out of his mouth cometh knowledge and understanding.*"—PROVERBS ii. 6.

> "Deep in unfathomable mines
> Of never-failing skill,
> He treasures up his bright designs.
> And works his sovereign will."—
> *Cowper.*

"Wisdom is the olive that springeth from the heart, bloometh on the tongue, and beareth fruit in the actions."—*Grymeston.*

---

23. "*God is with thee in all that thou doest.*"—GENESIS xxi. 22.

> "Brief is the record, but how full of bliss !
> What more ennobling word
> Can truth write on a mortal's tomb than this—
> 'He trusted in the Lord'?"—
> *T. H. Clark.*

"I cannot but take notice of the wonderful love of God to mankind, who, in order to encourage obedience to his laws, has annexed a present as well as a future reward to a good life."—*Melmoth.*

---

24. "*O man, who art thou that repliest against God? Shall the thing formed say to Him that formed it, Why hast Thou made me thus?*"—ROMANS ix. 20.

> "A father's voice with reverence we
> On earth have often heard ;
> The Father of our spirits now
> Demands the same regard."

"Do not search into the essence of the Divine nature ; for thou art impious, wishing to know what God hath not revealed."—*Menander.*

25. *"To him that knocketh it shall be opened."*—MATTHEW vii. 8.

"Come, my soul, thy suit prepare ;
    Jesus loves to answer prayer :
    He himself has bid thee pray,
    Therefore will not say thee nay."—

                     Newton.

"Because God is love, and desires to dwell in others, He has opened his heart unto all creatures, and poured forth unto them as much of his goodness and beauty as they were able to receive."—*Tholuck.*

26. *"Brethren, if a man be overtaken in a fault, ye which are spiritual restore such an one in the spirit of meekness: considering thyself lest thou also be tempted."*—GALATIANS vi. 1.

"Thou art the Spirit of all love,
    The Friend of kindly life,
    Though would'st not that our hearts should prove
    The pangs of wrath and strife."—

                     Gerhardt.

"Always say a kind word if you can, if only that it may come in, perhaps, with singular opportuneness, entering some mournful man's darkened room."—*Sir A. Helps.*

27. *"A little that a righteous man hath is better than the riches of many wicked."*—PSALM xxxvii. 16.

"All I ask for is, enough ;
    Only, when the way is rough,
    Let thy rod and staff impart
    Strength and courage to my heart."—

                     Conder.

"If you are but content, you have enough to live upon with comfort."—*Plautus.*

28. *" Take with you words, and turn to the Lord : say unto Him, Take away all iniquity and receive us graciously."* —HOSEA xiv. 2.

> " Go to thy home : thy father's heart
> Waits thee with welcome there :
> Go to thy God ! He'll grace impart ;
> 'Tis He who answers prayer."

" For weak, poor, helpless, unworthy though we be in ourselves, in *Him*, our Lord, our Redeemer, we are complete in the fullest, broadest, and most varied sense of that mighty word."—*Spurgeon.*

29. *" God is not unrighteous to forget your work and labour of love which ye have showed toward his name."*— HEBREWS vi. 10.

> " Be sure—no earnest work
> Of any honest creature, howbeit weak,
> Imperfect, ill-adapted, fails so much,
> It is not gathered as a grain of sand
> To enlarge the sum of human action used
> For carrying out God's end."

" If we dwelt more upon God's fulness, and his desire to make us partakers of it, our Christian character would be richer. God never reveals Himself to us as a distant glimmering light."—*Beecher.*

30. *" Behold I am with thee and will keep thee in all places whither thou goest."*—GENESIS xxviii. 15.

> " God is a King for ever,
> His kingdom ne'er shall cease ;
> His own shall He deliver,
> And bless them aye with peace."

" Nothing is superior to God : He must therefore govern the world. God is subject to no principle in nature, therefore He rules the whole of nature."—*Cicero.*

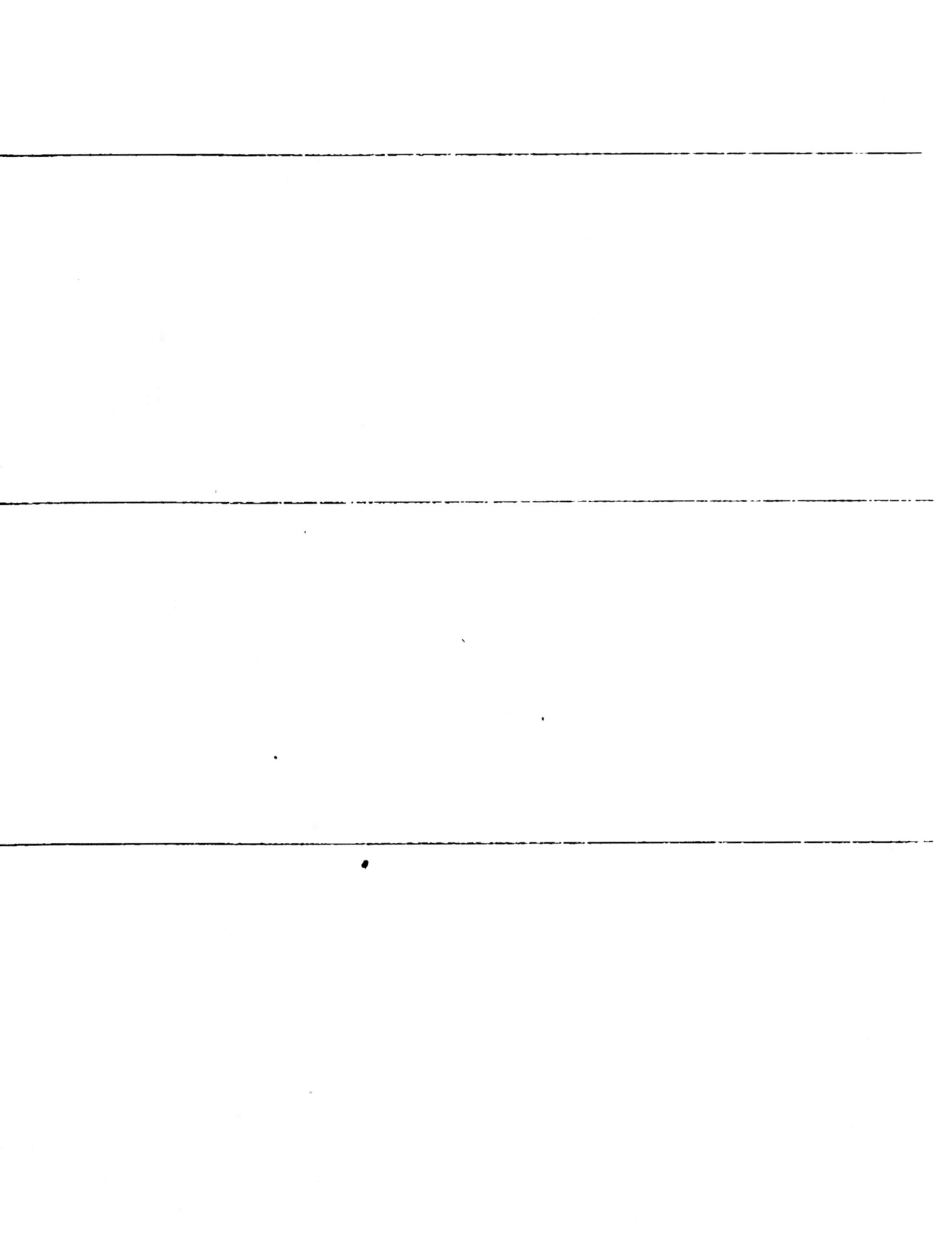

1. *"Christ is the end of the law for righteousness to every one that believeth."*—ROMANS x. 4.

" Father, in Thy mysterious presence kneeling,
　　Fain would our souls feel all thy kindling love,
　For we are weak, and need some deep revealing
　　Of trust, and strength, and calmness from above."—

S. Johnson.

" All that we mean by the heavenly joy and perfection is nothing but the restoration and the everlasting bloom of that high capacity for God, in which our normal state began, and of which that first state was only the germ, or prophecy."—*Bushnell.*

2. *"Jacob served seven years for Rachel; and they seemed unto him but a few days, for the love he had to her."*—GENESIS xxix. 20.

" Hearts are firm, though nerves be shaken,
　　When from Thee new life is taken :
　　Truth recruits itself by love ;
　　O what wine is there like love ?"—

Lynch.

" The great antique Heart : how like a child's in its simplicity, like a man's in its solemnity and depth."—*Carlyle.*

3. *"Bear ye one another's burdens, and so fulfil the law of Christ."*—GALATIANS vi. 2.

" To bear for them the cross, as if for Thee,
　　Strengthen me ever !
　Among thy hidden ones O number me,
　　Now, and for ever !"

" Difficulty is a severe instructor, set over us by the supreme ordinance of a parental Guardian and Legislator, who knows us better than we know ourselves ; and He loves us better too."—*Burke.*

43

4. *" Christ is not entered into the holy places made with hands,*
which are the figures of the true; but into heaven itself,
now to appear in the presence of God for us."—HEBREWS
ix. 24.

> " Thou seest our weakness, Lord !
> Our hearts are known to Thee :
> O ! lift Thou up the sinking hand,
> Confirm the feeble knee !"—
>
> *Gerhardt.*

" Some things God will bring to pass, and others will be unaccomplished, according to his will."—*Homer.*

---

5. *" Not every one that saith unto Me, Lord, Lord, shall enter*
into my kingdom; but he that doeth the will of my Father
which is in heaven."—MATTHEW vii. 21.

> " ' What shall I do to gain eternal life ?'
> Discharge aright
> The simple dues with which each day is rife—
> Yea, with thy might."—
>
> *Schiller.*

" For whatever a man's desire is, and whatsoever he may be as to
his soul, such every one becomes in a great measure."—*Plato.*

---

6. *David said, " I have been young, and now am old; yet have I*
not seen the righteous forsaken, nor his seed begging bread."
—PSALM xxxvii. 25.

> " Then, then, I feel that He,
> Remember'd or forgot,
> The Lord, is never far from me,
> Though I perceive Him not."—
>
> *Montgomery.*

" Godliness makes a man do everthing strongly and mightily ;
and whatever might take a man off from duty, or distract or distrust
him in it, all falls to nothing before this power."—*Dell.*

44

7.   *" How forcible are right words."*—JOB VI. 25.

" But God loves the constant cry ;
He wills the words should never die
That speak our needs.— Prayer pushes prayer
Up into heaven's sublimer air."

" He who seldom speaks, and with one calm well-timed word can strike dumb the loquacious, is a genius or a hero."—*Lavater.*

---

8. *" Whosoever believeth on Him shall not be ashamed."*—
ROMANS x. 11.

" There's no condemnation, the Pharisees own,
To those who hold out to the end ;
But the strongest would fall, and hold out not at all,
But as held by Jehovah's own hand."—

        D. Herbert.

" Faith is the root of all good works."—*Bishop Wilson.*

---

9. *" Trust in the Lord with all thine heart; and lean not unto thine own understanding."*—PROVERBS iii. 5.

" When He folds the cloud about Him,
Firm within it stands his throne ;
Wherefore should his children doubt Him,
Those to whom his love is known ?
God is with us, God is with us ;
We are never left alone."—

        Lynch.

" God is the light, which, never seen itself, makes all things visible."—*Richter.*

45

10. *"I the Lord thy God will hold thy right hand, saying unto thee, Fear not; I will help thee."*—ISAIAH xli. 13.

> " Stay with us, Lord ! and with Thy light,
> Illume the soul's abyss ;
> Scatter the darkness of our night,
> And fill the world with bliss."—
>
> *St. Bernard.*

" Godliness makes a man invincible from all evils and enemies, because all the power against him is but the power of the creature, but the power in him is the power of God."—*Dell.*

---

11. *" Let us hold fast the profession of our faith without wavering (for He is faithful that promised)."*—HEBREWS x. 23.

> " Who would build up his manhood well
> Must lay the great foundation-stone
> In piety, for he shall dwell
> Secure in that alone."

" None live so easily, so pleasantly, as those that live by faith." – *Matthew Henry.*

---

12. *" He cast out the spirits with his word, and healed all that were sick."*—MATTHEW viii. 16.

> " Thou, who didst come to bring
> On thy redeeming wing
> Healing and light,
> Health to the sick in mind,
> Light to the inly blind,
> Oh, now to all mankind
> Let there be light !"

" Even in war, moral power is to physical as three parts out of four."—*Napoleon I.*

13. "*All the while my breath is in me, and the spirit of God is in my nostrils; my lips shall not speak wickedness, nor my tongue utter deceit.*"—JOB xxvii. 3-4.

"God of my health ! I would Thy praise proclaim,
 And tell to earth and heaven Thy wondrous name,
 Declare the transports of my thankful breast,
 And say to all the world that I am blest."—

        From A. Monod.

"Consecration is going out into the world where God Almighty is, and using every power for his glory."—*Beecher.*

---

14. "*I know that, whatsoever God doeth, it shall be for ever: nothing can be put to it, nor anything taken from it.*"—ECCLESIASTES iii. 14.

"Tarry his leisure, then,
 Although He seem to stay ;
A moment's intercourse with Him,
 Thy grief will overpay."—

       Toplady.

"God is Alpha and Omega in the great world ; endeavour to make Him so in the little world ; make Him thy evening epilogue and thy morning prologue."—*Quarles.*

---

15. "*With Thee is the fountain of life: in Thy light shall we see light.*"—PSALM xxxvi. 9.

"O Thou, who art enrobed in light,
 How pure the soul must be,
When, placed within thy searching sight,
It shrinks not, but with calm delight
 Can live and look on Thee."

"Christian life consists in faith and charity."—*Luther.*

16. *" Be not wise in thine own eyes : fear the Lord, and depart from evil."*—PROVERBS iii. 7.

" God is not importunate :
    If we will not hear his voice
He is silent, and withdraws :
    Angels mourn, and fiends rejoice.
        O Lord, direct us !"—

S. Williams.

" The end of wisdom is consultation and deliberation."— *Demosthenes.*

---

17. *" Faith cometh by hearing, and hearing by the word of God."*— ROMANS x. 17.

" O holy Saviour, Friend unseen,
    The faint, the weak, on Thee may lean :
Help me, throughout life's varying scene,
    By faith to cling to Thee !"—

C. Elliott.

" Works without faith are like a fish without water ; it wants the element it should live in."—*Feltham.*

---

18. *" Jesus, knowing their thoughts, said, Wherefore think ye evil in your hearts ?"*—MATTHEW ix. 4.

" Yet high above the limits of my seeing,
    And folded far within the inmost heart,
And deep below the deeps of conscious being,
    Thy splendour shineth ; there, O God, Thou art."—

E. Scudder.

" Our spirit is often led astray by its own delusions."—*Voltaire.*

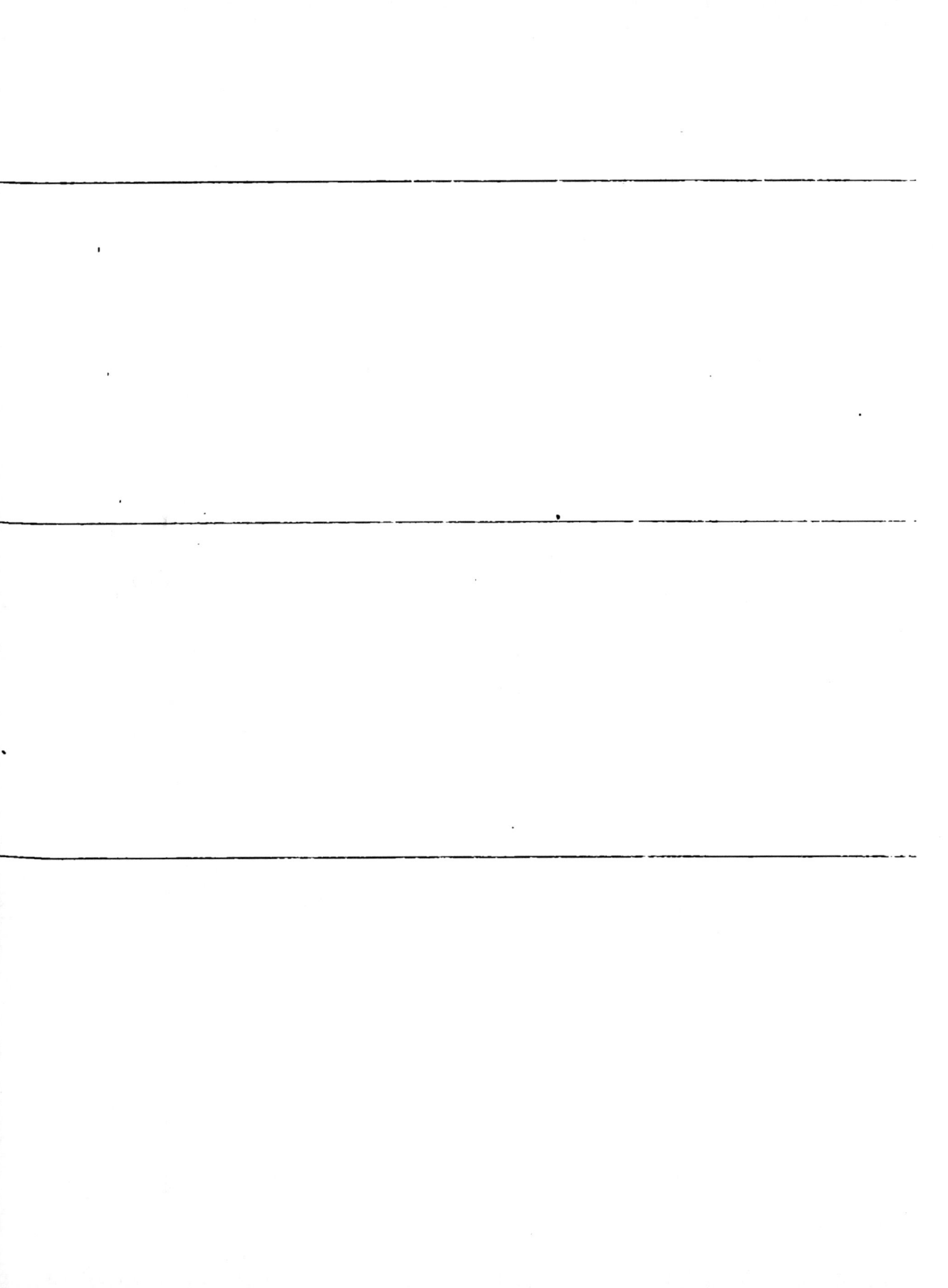

19. *" Wilt thou not from this time cry unto Me, My Father, Thou art the guide of my youth ?"*—JEREMIAH iii. 4.

> " Still on his plighted love
> At all events rely ;
> The very hidings of his face,
> Shall train thee up to joy."—
>
> *Toplady.*

" The fairest flower in the garden of creation is a young mind offering and unfolding itself to the influence of Divine wisdom."— *Sir J. Smith.*

20. *" Seek good, and not evil, that ye may live : and so the Lord, the God of hosts, shall be with you."*—AMOS v. 14.

> " Of good and pious works Thou art the seed
> That quickens only where Thou sayest it may :
> Unless Thou show to us thy own true way,
> No man can find it.   Father !   Thou must lead."—
>
> *M. Angelo.*

" Your name, your deeds, will be as legible on the hearts you leave behind as the stars on the brow of evening."—*Chalmers.*

21. *" Behold God is mighty, and despiseth not any : He is mighty in strength and wisdom."*—JOB xxxvi. 5.

> " Without thy presence earth gives no refection,
> Without thy presence sea affords no treasure,
> Without thy presence air is rank infection ;
> Without thy presence heaven itself no pleasure."—
>
> *Quarles.*

" Little facts and circumstances, in the economy of Almighty God, have irresistible charms for me, and serve, like others more prominent, to show the perfect and beautiful manner in and for which everything has been created."—*Jesse.*

22. "*A good name is better than precious ointment.*"—ECCLESIASTES
vii. I.

"O may our feet pursue the way
Our pious fathers led ;
With love and holy zeal obey
The counsels of the dead."—

Watts.

"He that is a good man is three-quarters of his way towards the
being a good Christian, wheresoever he lives, or whatsoever he is
called."—*South.*

23. "*Be not highminded.*"—ROMANS xi. 20.

"Rejoice, O young man ! in thy pride of life,
Sing, seer ! the songs that will not come again;
But know that still for these the judgment waits,
And God shall hold thee steward of thy pain."—

S. Williams.

"Take some quiet sober moment of life, and add together the two
ideas of pride and man ; behold him, creature of a span high,
stalking through infinite space in all the grandeur of littleness."—
S. Smith.

24. "*The word of the Lord is right, and all his works are done
in truth.*"—PSALM xxxiii. 4.

"Whate'er my God ordains is right ;
My light, my life is He,
Who cannot will me ought but good ;
I trust Him utterly."

"Everything is good when it comes from the hand of the
Almighty Creator ; everything degenerates in the hand of man."—
Rousseau.

25. "*If a man think himself to be something, when he is nothing, he deceiveth himself.*"—GALATIANS vi. 3.

"Discreetly may we guard our life
From faults which its professions mock;
But boldly stand in error's strife
And meet proud contradiction's shock."—
Lynch.

"A proud man is a fool in fermentation, that swells and boils over like a porridge-pot."—*Butler.*

---

26. "*I am merciful, saith the Lord, and I will not keep anger for ever. Only acknowledge thine iniquity.*"—JEREMIAH iii. 12-13.

"This is the way I long have sought,
And mourned because I found it not;
My grief, my burden, long have been
Because I could not cease from sin."—
Cennick.

"Repentance hath a purifying power, and every tear is of a cleansing virtue."—*South.*

---

27. "*The Lord by wisdom hath founded the earth; by understanding hath He established the heavens.*"—PROVERBS iii. 19.

"He sendeth sun, He sendeth shower;
Alike they're needful for the flower:
And joys and tears alike are sent
To give the soul fit nourishment."—
Adams.

"The world is a beautiful book, but of little use to him who cannot read it."—*Galdoni.*

28. *"Jesus said, Daughter, be of good comfort; thy faith hath made thee whole. And the woman was made whole from that hour."*—MATTHEW ix. 22.

> " Did ever sinner plead with Thee,
> And Thou reject his lowly plea ?
> Does not thy word still pledged remain
> That none shall seek thy face in vain ?"

" Faith in God hallows and confirms the union between parents and children, subjects and rulers."—*Pestalozzi.*

29. *" Let us consider one another to provoke unto love and to good works."*—HEBREWS x. 24.

> " One is wise
> To know, another strong to do, a third
> To love or suffer patiently ;—yet all,
> Resembling separate stars in sphere remote,
> In their combined action, each with each,
> Together make one firmament."—
> *Mudie.*

" Good deeds will shine as the stars of heaven."—*Chalmers.*

30. *" He that giveth, let him do it with simplicity; he that ruleth, with diligence; he that showeth mercy, with cheerfulness."*—ROMANS xii. 8.

> " The heads that guide endue with skill ;
> The hands that work preserve from ill ;
> That we, who these foundations lay,
> May lay the top-stone in its day."

" The manner of giving shows the character of the giver more than the gift itself."—*Lavater.*

31. "*The Lord looketh from heaven; He beholdeth all the sons of men.*"—PSALM xxxiii. 13.

"Lord, how can I, whose native sphere
Is dark, whose mind is dim,
Before thy radiant light appear,
And on my naked spirit bear
Thine uncreated beam?"

"Ah! there is a great deal of craft and cunning among men—they are very shrewd and subtle, and can go far and long in artifice and duplicity : but God is a match for them all."—*Beecher.*

1.   *" Thou God seest me."*—GENESIS xvi. 13.

" Dissolve the cold which chills my heart,
The warming beams of light impart,
   Enliven every power :
Oh ! let the dew of grace distil ;
My soul with heavenly virtues fill,
   And guard it every hour."

" When we sin, we are not going against a cold, unfeeling law ; but are striking with cruel hand, direct at the living, loving heart of God."—*Beecher.*

2.   *" If ye forgive men their trespasses, your heavenly Father will also forgive you."*—MATTHEW vi. 14.

" Thy promise is my only plea,
   With this I venture nigh ;
Thou callest burden'd souls to Thee,
   And such, O Lord, am I."—

Newton.

" If thou art able, correct by teaching those who sin ; but if thou art unable, remember that indulgence is given to thee."—*M. Aurelius.*

3.   *" As many as are led by the Spirit of God, they are the sons of God."*—ROMANS viii. 14.

" Each promise is sure
   That shines in his word,
And tells me, though poor,
   I'm rich in the Lord."

" God is in all things and places alike, and is ever alike, ready to give Himself to us, in so far as we are able to receive Him ; and he knows God aright who sees Him in everything."—*Tauler.*

4. *"Now we, brethren, as Isaac was, are the children of promise."*
—GALATIANS iv. 28.

"Even as thou wilt, so be it unto thee,
Thy heart the measure of the grace shall be,
From My rich store supplied."

"We know much of heaven, if it be but in the initials and rudiments, wherein, in the lively characters of love, peace, joy, and devout conformity to his will, God's finger has traced it in the regenerate soul."—*D. Greenwell.*

---

5. *"Exhort one another daily, while it is called To-day; lest any of you be hardened through the deceitfulness of sin."*—
HEBREWS iii. 13.

"Aid the dawning, tongue and pen; aid it, hopes of honest men;
Aid it, paper, aid it, type; aid it, for the hour is ripe,—
And our earnest must not slacken into play:
Men of thought and men of action, clear the way."

"In a truly godlike man his love is pure and unmixed, and full of kindness, insomuch that he cannot but love in sincerity all men and things, and wish well and do good to them and rejoice in their welfare."

---

6. *"Create in me a clean heart, O God; and renew a right spirit within me."*—PSALM li. 10.

"Oh, ne'er may our forgetful hearts
O'erlook thy bounteous care;
But what our Father's hand imparts
Still own in praise and prayer."

"As a ray of light in a pure drop of water is divided into seven colours, so it is with love in a pure heart, it divides into more than sevenfold virtue; yea, rather, all virtue springs from it alone."—*Tholuck.*

55

---

7. *" My Lord, if now I have found favour in thy sight, pass not away, I pray Thee, from thy servant."*—GENESIS xviii. 3.

> " Spirit of God ! Almighty One,
> Sent from the Father and the Son,
> Completer of their work begun,
> Good Spirit, hear and aid."—
>
> *Prichard.*

" How little of our deepest impressions can be given in words ; how much must be for ever left unsaid."—*Haweis.*

---

8. *" Appear not unto men to fast."*—MATTHEW vi. 18.

> " Prevent me, lest I harbour pride,
> Lest I in my own strength confide ;
> Show me my weakness ; let me see
> I have my pow'r, my all, from Thee."

" Understandest thou how much easier it is to be a pious visionary than to act an honest part in life ?"—*Lessing.*

---

9. *" Hear Thou from heaven thy dwelling place, and forgive, and render unto every man according unto all his ways, whose heart Thou knowest."*—II CHRONICLES vi. 30.

> " Love me, O Lord, forgivingly,
> O ever be my friend ;
> And still, when Thou reprovest me,
> Reproof with pity blend."—
>
> *Lynch.*

" It is in vain for you to expect, it is impudent for you to ask of God, forgiveness on your own behalf, if you refuse to exercise this forgiving temper with respect to others."—*Hoadley.*

JUNE.

---

10. *"Speak to the earth, and it shall teach thee."*—JOB xii. 8.

> " For the strength of the hills we bless Thee,
>   Our God, our Father's God.—
> Thou hast made thy children mighty
>   By the touch of the mountain sod."

" Only let us love God, and then nature will compass us about like a cloud of divine witnesses, and all influences from the earth, and things on the earth, will be ministers of God to do us good."—*Euthanasy.*

---

11. *"Let us run with patience the race that is set before us, looking unto Jesus the author and finisher of our faith."*—HEBREWS xii. 1-2.

> " I know that Thou wilt make my grief to cease,
>   Wilt send the cool, soft drops of healing rain,
>   And make my scarred heart green with springing grain,
> That after patient waiting cometh peace."

" One glance at the cross would make us pause at the pursuit of the bauble, bring confusion on the face at daring to be sensual."—*Melvill.*

---

12. *"Fear thou not; for I am with thee: be not dismayed; for I am thy God: I will strengthen thee."*—ISAIAH xli. 10.

> " Our only God Thou art ;
>   Our strength is all of Thee ;
> Uphold each fearful heart,
>   Confirm each feeble knee."

" The true disciple of Jesus needs not to forget himself in order to be cheerful in his very innermost soul. The present day may have its storms, but the future only smiles the more brightly to him."—*Zschokke.*

13. " *Trust in the Lord, and do good; so shalt thou dwell in the land, and verily thou shalt be fed.*"—PSALM xxxvii. 3.

> " Bless, Lord, my going out,
> And bless my coming in ;
> Keep off all evil from without,
> And make me pure within."

" The virtue of a man ought to be measured not by his extraordinary exertions, but by his every-day conduct."—*Pascal.*

14. " *A good man out of the good treasure of the heart bringeth forth good things.*"—MATTHEW xii. 35.

> " Oh help us, Lord ! each hour of need,
> Thy heavenly succour give ;
> Help us in thought, and word, and deed,
> Each hour on earth we live !"—
>
> *Milman.*

" A wise man will so act that whatever he does may rather seem voluntary and of his own free will than done by compulsion."—*Machiavelli.*

15. " *Envy thou not the oppressor, and choose none of his ways.*"— PROVERBS iii. 31.

> " The Lord receives his highest praise
> From humble minds and hearts sincere ;
> While all the loud professor says
> Offends the righteous Judge's ear."—
>
> *Cowper.*

" How unbecoming it is for one that is mortal to entertain proud, aspiring thoughts : for presumption, when it has put forth the blade, is wont to produce for fruit an all-mournful harvest of woe."—*Æschylus.*

16. "*If it be possible, as much as lieth in you, live peaceably with all men.*"—ROMANS xii. 18.

"Brave minds, howe'er at war, are secret friends,
Their generous discord with the battle ends ;
In peace they wonder whence dissension rose,
And ask how souls so like could e'er be foes."—
Tickell.

"Courtesy is a science of the highest importance. It is like grace and beauty in the body, which charm at first sight."—*Montaigne.*

---

17. "*Thou shalt call me, My Father ; and shalt not turn away from me.*"—JEREMIAH iii. 19.

"And I am His.—Oh heart, be faithful still !
Still let Him lead me as it seems Him best !
With Him to combat, or with Him to rest,
March, or encamp, according to his will."

"Truly to love God we must know Him—know Him as our Father, as our best, truest, nearest Friend : feel Him near to us in every bright and joyous, and in every clouded and trying scene of life."

---

18. "*As we have therefore opportunity, let us do good unto all men.*"—GALATIANS vi. 10.

"Let us live, O Lord, at one,
As Thou with the Father art ;
That through all the world be none
Of thy members left apart."

"Christian love is not to be limited by any boundaries of our own invention, but, like the sun, which shines upon the evil and the good, it is to be co-extensive with humanity itself."—*Crombie.*

19. *" Though a sinner do evil an hundred times, and his days be prolonged, yet surely I know that it shall be well with them that fear God."*—ECCLESIASTES viii. 12.

> " Still wait in faith, for nought is dead
>   Of all that thou hast sown :
> Be not a child who roots up seeds
>   To *see* that they have grown."—
>
> *Powers.*

" For God rewards good done in this world, even here also."—*Lessing.*

20. *" By thy words thou shalt be justified, and by thy words thou shalt be condemned."*—MATTHEW xii. 37.

> " Grant me to rule my inner life aright,
>   And act and speak as ever in thy sight,
> A friend to all true virtue, but a foe
>   To all Thou hatest."

" What you keep by you you can change and mend : but words spoke can never be recalled."—*Roscommon.*

21. *" What doth the Lord require of thee, but to do justly, and to love mercy, and to walk humbly with thy God?"*—MICAH vi. 8.

> " We have not wings, we cannot soar :
>   But we have feet to scale and climb,
> By slow degrees, by more and more,
>   The cloudy summits of our time."

" Guilt and sin separate the soul from God as the widest wastes of untravelled space could never separate. Remove these, and the distance is at once annihilated."—*Dr. Caird.*

22. *" Commit thy way unto the Lord; trust also in Him; and He shall bring it to pass."*—PSALM xxxvii. 5.

> " Wait upon his mercies ;
> Pray, and look on high :
> For a gracious answer
> Will come by and by."—
>
> *Monsell.*

" Be convinced, therefore, that you are invited and allowed by Jesus, not merely that you may be happy in heaven, but that, by doing his will, the earth may once more be transformed into a paradise."—*Krummacher.*

23. *" Follow peace with all men, and holiness, without which no man shall see the Lord."*—HEBREWS xii. 14.

> " Thou art the true, the only source
> Whence concord comes to men ;
> Oh, that thy power might have free course,
> And bring us peace again !"—
>
> *Gerhardt.*

" Yea, if a man were to suffer himself to be torn in pieces, and did not learn to cleanse himself thoroughly from his sins, to behave towards his fellow-creatures in a spirit of generous love, and to love God above all things, it would be useless and in vain."—*Tauler.*

24. *" Take fast hold of instruction; let her not go: keep her ; for she is thy life."*—PROVERBS iv. 13.

> " Thou canst make me understand,
> Though I am slow of heart,—
> Thine, in whom I live and move,
> Thine the work, the power is thine ;
> Thou art wisdom, power, and love ;
> And all Thou art is mine."—
>
> *C. Wesley.*

" The tree of knowledge is grafted upon the tree of life."—*Sir H. Davy.*

25. *"Be not overcome of evil, but overcome evil with good."*—
ROMANS xii. 21.

" Lord ! each thought and inclination,
 All my heart and will inspire,
That my soul, thy new creation,
 Thee may serve with pure desire."—
A. T. Russell.

" Goodness I call the habit, and goodness of nature the inclination. This, of all virtues and dignities of the mind, is the greatest,
being the character of the Deity."—*Bacon.*

---

26. *"He that received seed into the good ground is he that
heareth the word, and understandeth it."*—MATTHEW xiii. 23.

" Oh let my thoughts, my actions, and my will
 Obedient solely to thy impulse move,
My heart and senses keep Thou blameless still,
 Fix'd and absorbed in God's unuttered love."

" The improvement of the understanding is for two ends : first
our own increase of knowledge ; secondly, to enable us to believe
and make out that knowledge to others."—*Locke.*

---

27. *"Let him that glorieth glory in this, that he understandeth
and knoweth me, that I am the Lord which exercise lovingkindness, judgment, and righteousness, in the earth."*—
JEREMIAH ix. 24.

" In every object here I see
 Something, O Lord, that leads to Thee :
Firm as the rocks thy promise stands,
 Thy mercies, countless as the sands :
Thy love, a sea immensely wide ;
 Thy grace, an overflowing tide."—*Newton.*

" We often pass on blindly when He desires to give us his richest
and most glorious revelations ; often we are unable to understand
what He means ; when He addresses us with his deep, spiritual
words."—*Hossbach.*

28. *" The Lord is good, a stronghold in the day of trouble; and He knoweth them that trust in Him."*—NAHUM i. 7.

" Never doubt His promise,
Or faith's full reward.
Wait, I say, in patience,
Wait upon the Lord."—

Monsell.

" Suffering well borne is better than suffering removed.—When we reach the garden above, we shall find that out of those very wounds over which we sighed and groaned on earth, have sprung verdant branches, bearing precious fruit."—*Beecher.*

29. *Jesus said, " In the world ye shall have tribulation : but be of good cheer; I have overcome the world."*—JOHN xvi. 33.

" Our very perils shut us in
To thy supporting care.
We venture on the awful deep,
And find our courage there."—

Waring.

" Against these hindrances we cannot even strive, much less rise above them, unless the Comforter be continually helping us onward, by convincing us more and more deeply of the sin of not believing in Christ."—*Hare.*

30. *" Lord, all my desire is before Thee; and my groaning is not hid from Thee."*—PSALM xxxviii. 9.

" To Thee I bring my care,
The care I cannot flee ;
Thou wilt not only share,
But take it all for me.
O, loving Saviour, now to Thee,
I bring the load that wearies me."—

Havergal.

" The reason why there are so many phases, or seeming lapses, in Christian experience, is, not because it is false, but oftener because it is genuine."—*Bushnell.*

JULY.

1. *" Whosoever will, let him take the water of life freely."—*
REVELATION xxii. 17.
" Why art thou cast down, O my soul?
Uplift thee, and be strong :
Thy care upon thy Maker roll ;
Thy sadness doth Him wrong.—
The God who rules above,
His child doth know and love."—*Oberlin.*

" Believing in Him who is the only propitiation for the sins of the world, you are not only delivered from guilt, but brought into such sympathy with the heart of the great Sufferer, that you regard sin with feelings that are the reflection of his own."—*Dr. Caird.*

---

2.   *" Keep yourselves from idols."—*1 JOHN v. 21.
" Lead, kindly Light, amid the encircling gloom,
Lead Thou me on.
The night is dark, and I am far from home ;
Lead Thou me on.
Keep Thou my feet ; I do not ask to see
The distant scene ; one step enough for me."—
Newman.

" The germ of idolatry is contained in the proneness of man's feelings and imagination to take their impressions from outward objects, rather than from the dictates of reason."—*Hare.*

---

3. *" This is the confidence that we have in Him, that, if we ask anything according to his will, He heareth us."—*
1 JOHN v. 14.
" By his goodness, and his meekness,
By his grace in deed and word ;
By his power in mortal weakness,
He is worthy to be heard."

" All between these two magnificent notes rolls the anthem of God's mercy—' *Whosoever will.*' That is, the beginning and the ending."—*Beecher.*

64

4. *"Add to your faith, virtue; and to virtue, knowledge."*—
2 PETER i. 5.

"Come let us anew our journey pursue,
    Roll round with the year,
And never stand still till the Master appear.
His adorable will let us gladly fulfil,
    And our talents improve,
By the patience of hope, and the labour of love."

"The height of all philosophy, both natural and moral, is to know thy selfe; and the end of this knowledge is, to know God."— *Quarles.*

5. *"Surely his salvation is nigh them that fear Him."*—
PSALM lxxxv. 9.

"Gentle Jesus, O how blessed
    He who flies this world for Thee!
His the breast whose state is ever
    Calm, serene, and spirit free."

"God did not create spirits, and endow them with a knowledge of Himself, to allow them to forget Him after a brief space. He did not unite souls by the spiritual bonds of love, to separate them again for ever."—*Zschokke.*

6. *"Keep yourselves in the love of God, looking for the mercy of our Lord Jesus Christ."*—JUDE 21.

"Though I am dark, Thou seest me,
    And knowest all my sins;
I cannot hide one thought from Thee,
Nor would I, Lord; oh search and see
    All that lies hid within."

"Some glances of real beauty may be seen in their faces who dwell in true meekness. There is a harmony in the sound of that voice to which divine love gives utterance."—*Woolman.*

7. *" The Lord grant you that ye may find rest."*—RUTH i. 9.

> " O Shepherd, Shepherd, merciful and mild,
>   Hear Thou thy child.—
>   O heal the sick sore heart,—lest it quite break,—
>   For Thy name's sake."—
>
> *Wilson.*

" There is a power in this rest in God, of which the men who are rushing along the broad and dusty highway can form no conception. The meadows on which the soul refreshes itself are ever green."—*Tholuck.*

8. *" Thou hast been a strength to the poor, a strength to the needy in his distress, a refuge from the storm, a shadow from the heat."*—ISAIAH xxv. 4.

> " Our Advocate with God,
>   He undertakes our cause,
>   And spreads through all the earth abroad
>   The victory of the cross."

" The perfect love of God knoweth no difference between the poor and the rich."—*Pacuvius.*

9. *" The lips of the righteous feed many."*—PROVERBS x. 21.

> " Spirit of sacred happiness,
>   Who makest energy delight,
>   And love to be in weakness might ;
>   Now with enlivening impulse bless,
>   Now re-confirm our steadfastness,
>   And make us vigorous and bright."—
>
> *Lynch.*

" Holiness is something of God, wherever it is. It is an efflux from Him, and lives in Him ; as the sunbeams, although they gild this lower world, and spread their golden wings over us, yet they are not so much here where they shine, as in the sun from whence they flow."—*Cudworth.*

10. "*Rend your heart, and not your garments, and turn unto the Lord your God: for He is gracious and merciful, slow to anger, and of great kindness.*"—JOEL ii. 13.

"And shall the voice of mercy plead in vain,
    In the world's gaudy glare?
Can the touch'd heart, grown doubly hard again,
    Forget the answered prayer?"—
                                T. H. Clark.

"The more honesty a man has, the less he affects the air of a saint. The affectation of sanctity is a blotch on the face of piety."—*Lavater.*

11. "*There shall be no night There; and they need no candle, neither light of the sun; for the Lord God giveth them light.*"—REVELATION xxii. 5.

"Although its features fade in light of unimagined bliss,
We have shadowy revealings of the better world, in this."—

"The material world has its links, by which it is made to shake hands, as it were, with the vegetable—the vegetable with the animal—the animal with the intellectual—and the intellectual with what we may be allowed to hope of the angelic."—*Colton.*

12. "*I will hear what God the Lord will speak: for He will speak peace unto his people.*"—PSALM lxxxv. 8.

"Let us go and learn His meaning,
    When He says to man 'I know;'
Let us, on His bosom leaning,
    See what He came down to show."

"God is where the sun glows, God is where the violet blooms, is where yon bird is flapping its wings, is where this worm is moving. Though no friend, no man, be with thee, fear nothing! God is here."—*Dinter.*

13. *"Avoid foolish questions, and genealogies, and contentions, and strivings about the law; for they are unprofitable and vain."*—TITUS iii. 9.

> " Teach us to count our short'ning days,
> And with true diligence apply
> Our hearts to wisdom's sacred ways,
> That we may learn to live—and die."

" In disputes about common things, as every one feels that he may be mistaken, stubbornness and obstinacy are never carried to an extreme ; but in those which we have respecting religion, as every one naturally feels sure that his opinion is the true one, we are highly indignant against those who, instead of changing, are bent on making us change."—*Montesqieu.*

14. *"Humble yourselves therefore under the mighty hand of God, that He may exalt you in due time."*—I PETER v. 6.

> " Creator Spirit, by whose aid
> The world's foundations first were laid,
> Come, visit every pious mind ;
> Come, pour Thy joys on human kind ;
> From sin and sorrow set us free,
> And make Thy temples worthy Thee."—*Dryden.*

"Humility is the first lesson we learn from reflection, and self-distrust the first proof we give of having obtained a knowledge of ourselves."—*Zimmerman.*

15. *"And this commandment have we from Him, That he who loveth God love his brother also."*—I JOHN iv. 21.

> " God fill thee with His heavenly light
> To steer thy Christian course aright ;
> Make thee a tree, of blessed root,
> That ever bends with godly fruit."—*J. C. Jacobi.*

"We can sometimes love what we do not understand, but it is impossible completely to understand what we do not love."—*Mrs. Jameson.*

16. *"Commit thy works unto the Lord, and thy thoughts shall be established."*—PROVERBS xvi. 3.

> " I cannot lose Thee ! still in Thee abiding,
> The end is clear, how wide soe'er I roam,
> The law that holds the worlds my steps is guiding,
> And I must rest at last in Thee, my Home."—
> *E. Scudder.*

" It is by suggesting certain motives, and predisposing the mind, that He excites the active powers of the will, or restrains them."— *Plutarch.*

---

17. *"Come, and let us go up to the mountain of the Lord, and to the house of the God of Jacob; and He will teach us of his ways, and we will walk in his paths."*—MICAH iv. 2.

> " With all the powers my poor soul hath
> Of humble love, and loyal faith,
> I come, dear Lord, to worship Thee,
> Whom too much love bowed down for me."—
> *Crawshaw.*

" God says the peace of a man who loves Him shall flow like a river. The man hears it when he rises in the morning; he hears it in the quiet noon; he hears it when the sun goes down; and if he wakes in the night, its sound is in his ears."—*Beecher.*

---

18. *"The Lord recompense thy work, and a full reward be given thee of the Lord God of Israel."*—RUTH ii. 12.

> " Teach us the things we ought to know;
> And may we find them true;
> And still, in stature as we grow,
> Increase in wisdom too."—
> *W. H. Bathurst.*

" All is vanity which is not honest, and there is no solid wisdom but in real piety."—*Evelyn.*

19. *" Trust ye in the Lord for ever : for in the Lord Jehovah is everlasting strength."*—ISAIAH xxvi. 4.

" Lord we have wandered long through doubt and sorrow,
    And Thou hast made each step an onward one ;
And we will trust for every unknown morrow ;
    Thou wilt sustain us till the work is done."—
                     S. Johnson.

" Between good men and God there is a friendship which virtue conciliates ; a friendship, do I say ? yea, a kindred and similitude."
—*Seneca.*

20. *" Talk no more so exceeding proudly ; let not arrogancy come out of your mouth : for the Lord is a God of knowledge, and by Him actions are weighed."*—I SAMUEL ii. 3.

" Take me, whom Thyself hast bought !
    Bring into captivity
Every high aspiring thought
    That would not stoop to Thee."—
                 C. Wesley.

" Pride is not only dreadfully mischievous in human society, but perhaps of all others, the most insuperable bar to real inward improvement."—*W. Carter.*

21. *" The Lord bless thee, and keep thee : the Lord make his face to shine upon thee, and be gracious unto thee."*—NUMBERS vi. 24, 25.

" In One who walked on earth a man of woe,
    Was holier peace than e'en this hour inspires.
From Him to me let inward quiet flow,
    And give the might my failing will requires."—
                 Sterling.

" To be without evil thoughts is God's best gift."—*Æschylus.*

70

22. *" Yea, all of you, be subject one to another, and be clothed with humility: for God resisteth the proud, and giveth grace to the humble."*—I PETER v. 5.

> " Whate'er consists not with thy love,
> O! teach me to resign!
> I'm rich to all th' intents of bliss,
> If Thou, O God, art mine."—
> *Toplady.*

" God looks to pure and not to full hands."—*P. Syrus.*

23. *" He that overcometh shall inherit all things; and I will be his God, and he shall be my son."*—REVELATION xxi. 7.

> " ' But enemies are round.'—Yes, child, I know
> That where thou least expect'st thou'lt find a foe;
> But victor thou shalt prove o'er all below—
> Only, seek strength above."

" Great works are performed not by strength, but by perseverance."—*Johnson.*

24. *" There is no fear in love; but perfect love casteth out fear."*—I JOHN iv. 18.

> " 'Tis not the skill of human art
> Which gives me power my God to know;
> The sacred lessons of the heart
> Come not from instruments below,
> Love is my teacher."—
> *Madame Guyon.*

" True love fears no winter. No, no! its spring *is* and ever remains."—*Tieck.*

25. *"Shew us thy mercy, O Lord, and grant us thy salvation."*
—PSALM lxxxv. 7.

"We want thy help, for we are frail ;
Thy light, for we are blind ;
Let grace o'er all our doubts prevail,
To prove that Thou art kind."

"God is right diligent to be with us at all seasons, and to teach us, that He may bring us to Himself when we are like to go astray."—*Tauler.*

26. *"Children's children are the crown of old men ; and the glory of children are their fathers."*—PROVERBS xvii. 6.

"Those children from our words and ways are gaining
A bias which will sway them to life's end ;
Traces they still will show of childhood's training,
When with the fading past our memories blend."—
Wilton.

"The more we learn of them, and the more we grow like them, the more we shall be able to teach them, and to draw from them the strength and comfort God designed them to give."—*S. Cox.*

27. *"The Lord God is my strength, and He will make my feet like hinds' feet, and He will make me to walk upon mine high places."*—HABAKKUK iii. 19.

"Hosannas to my God I'll raise,
Break forth, my heart, in joy and praise,
Break forth in happy song !
Lord, I am all too weak to sing,
I only stammer out, my King,
Thanks that to Thee belong."

"Praise is the reflection of virtue."—*Bacon.*

28. *"Blessed are ye that sow beside all waters."*—ISAIAH xxxii. 20.

> "Our hope, Lord, faileth never,
>   When Thou thy word dost plight :
> My fears then ceased for ever,
>   And all my soul was light."—
>
> *F. E. Cox.*

"Charity is the scope of all God's commands."—*Chrysostom.*

---

29. *"The Lord maketh poor, and maketh rich : He bringeth low, and lifteth up."*—1 SAMUEL ii. 7.

> "Thy presence makes celestial day,
>   And fills the raptur'd soul with bliss ;
> Night would prevail, were God away,
>   And spirits pine in paradise !
> In vain would all the angels try
> To fill thy room, thy lack supply."—
>
> *Simon Browne.*

"Omniscience and goodness, without a correspondent power, would be strangely short of satisfaction ; but when omnipotence comes into the notion, the grandeur is perfect and the pleasure entire."—*T. Collier.*

---

30. *"Feed the flock of God which is among you."*—1 PETER v. 2.

> "Leave me not, Lord, and I will be
>   A better servant unto Thee ;
> And what I have in zeal begun,
>   Shall with discretion too be done."—
>
> *Lynch.*

"Charity is an universal duty, which it is in every man's power sometimes to practise, since every degree of assistance given to another, upon proper motives, is an act of charity."—*Johnson.*

31. *" Behold I make all things new. And He said unto me, Write : for these words are true and faithful."*— REVELATION xxi. 5.

" Thou seemest human and divine,
  The highest, holiest manhood, Thou ;
  Our wills are ours, we know not how ;
Our wills are ours, to make them Thine."—

Tennyson.

" All event is God's arbitrament."—*Schiller.*

AUGUST.

1. *" Thou, Lord, art good, and ready to forgive; and plenteous in mercy unto all them that call upon Thee."*—PSALM lxxxvi. 5.

> " I cannot always here below
>   Sing out thy praises as I would ;
> The music will not always flow
>   As unto Thee it ever should."—
>
> Mason.

"O man immortal! live for something. Do good, and leave behind you a monument of virtue that the storm of time can never destroy. Write your name in kindness, love, and mercy, on the hearts you come in contact with year by year."—*Chalmers.*

---

2. *" Hitherto hath the Lord helped us."*—1 SAMUEL vii. 12.

> " I came to Jesus as I was,
>   Weary, and worn, and sad ;
> I found in Him a resting-place,
>   And He has made me glad."—
>
> Bonar.

" The river that has flowed hitherto must still flow on : the channel may be now wide and the current smooth, but once it was rapid, struggling against the rude rocks."—*Lynch.*

---

3. *" He that loveth not knoweth not God; for God is love."*— 1 JOHN iv. 8.

> " Wondrous woes that brought salvation !
>   Wondrous grace to sinners shown !
> Heaven is wrapt in contemplation
>   Of his love, whom men disown !
> Oh, my soul ! wilt thou disown Him ?
> Wilt thou not, my heart, enthrone Him ?"—
>
> Russell.

" Love is not altogether a delirium, yet it has many points in common therewith. I call it rather a discerning of the infinite in the finite—of the idea made real."—*Carlyle.*

4. *" Use hospitality one to another without grudging."* —
1 PETER iv. 9.

" O Holy Ghost ! Thou fire of love,
   Enkindle with Thy flame my will ;
Come with Thy strength, Lord, from above,
   Help me Thy bidding to fulfil."—

Angelus.

" There is an emanation from the heart in genuine hospitality which cannot be described, but is immediately felt, and puts the stranger at once at his ease."—*W. Irving.*

5. *" The work of righteousness shall be peace; and the effect of righteousness quietness and assurance for ever."*—
ISAIAH xxxii. 17.

" Oh for a closer walk with God !
   A calm and heavenly frame ;
   A light to shine upon the road
   That leads me to the Lamb."—

Cowper.

" Peace is the happy, natural state of man."—*Thomson.*

6. *" God shall wipe away all tears."*—REVELATION xxi. 4.

" O may I never grieve my Lord,
   My Lord who loves so well ;
   May fear of grieving Thee be more
   Than fear of flaming hell."

" Of all the created comforts, God is the lender ; you are the borrower, not the owner."—*Rutherford.*

7. *"The heart of the wise teacheth his mouth, and addeth learning to his lips."*—PROVERBS xvi. 23.

"Give me, O Lord, an earnest heart,
　　Anxious to do thy will :
Contented with whatever part
　　In life 'tis mine to fill."

" In our search after God and contemplation of Him our wisdom doth consist ; in our worship of God, and obedience to Him, our religion doth consist ; in both of them our happiness doth consist." —*Whichcote.*

8. *"The Lord is in his holy temple : let all the earth keep silence before Him."*—HABAKKUK ii. 20.

" Before Jehovah's awful throne,
　　Ye nations, bow with sacred joy ;
Know that the Lord is God alone,
　　He can create, and He destroy."—
　　　　　　　　　　　　　Watts.

"The created world is but a small parenthesis in eternity."— *Sir T. Browne.*

9. *"The Lord God is a sun and shield: the Lord will give grace and glory : no good thing will He withhold from them that walk uprightly."*—PSALM lxxxiv. 11.

" Hosanna ! Lord be Thou our help and friend,
　Thy aid to us in mercy send ;
　　That each may bring his soul
　　An offering unto Thee, unstain'd and whole.
　Thou wilt have none for thy disciples, Lord,
　But those who truly keep, not only hear thy word."—
　　　　　　　　　　　　　Schmolk.

" The superfluous blossoms on a fruit-tree are meant to symbolise the large way in which God loves to do pleasant things."—*Beecher.*

10. *" Turn not aside from following the Lord, but serve the Lord with all your heart."*—1 SAMUEL xii. 20.

> " Lord, Thou art good—we say it when
>   Thy fierce east breezes blow ;
> Lord, Thou art good—we still repeat
>   In thy soft summer glow ;
> And whether next day rain or shine,
> Shadow and sunshine, both are thine."—*I. Fyvie.*

" Divine Providence tempers his blessings to secure their better effect. He keeps our joys and our fears on an even balance, that we may neither presume nor despair."—*Wogan.*

---

11. *" As every man hath received the gift, even so minister the same one to another, as good stewards of the manifold grace of God."*—1 PETER iv. 10.

> " We pray for glad men and for grieved,
>   That, one another knowing,
> The sorrowful may be relieved,
>   The happy happier growing.
> For all who are for freedom bound,
>   For all who get to give,
> Or suffer wrong to strengthen right,
>   And die that men may live."—*Lynch.*

" In every occasion in which virtue is exercised, if something is not added to happiness, something is taken away from anxiety."—*Bentham.*

---

12. *" Take heed, brethren, lest there be in any of you an evil heart of unbelief."*—HEBREWS iii. 12.

> " Lord, draw reluctant souls
>   To seek a father's love ;
> Then shall attendant angels hear
>   The joyful news above."—*Dobell.*

" There is but one thing without honour ; smitten with eternal barrenness, inability to do or to be :—insincerity, unbelief."—*Carlyle.*

13. *"He that handleth a matter wisely, shall find good."—*
PROVERBS xvi. 20.

"Though to-day may not fulfil
All thy hopes, have patience still,
For perchance to-morrow's sun
Sees thy happier days begun."—
Gerhardt.

"Dare to be wise ; begin. He who puts off from hour to hour the act of living wisely, is like the rustic who sits waiting on the bank till the river floats past."—*Horace.*

14. *" The liberal deviseth liberal things; and by liberal things shall he stand."—*ISAIAH xxxii. 8.

" Meek and lowly, pure and holy,
Chief among the blessed three ;
Turning sadness into gladness,
Blessed art thou, Charity."

" Liberality consists less in giving much than in giving at the right moment."—*La Bruyère.*

15. *" Let us not love in word, neither in tongue; but in deed and in truth."—*1 JOHN iii. 18.

" Jesus, Thy love has found my heart,
And raised it up to Thee ;
Jesus, that love doth feast my soul,
'Tis present heaven to me."

" Sincerity is to speak as we think, to do as we pretend and profess, to perform and make good what we promise, and really to be what we would seem and appear to be."—*Tillotson.*

16. *"And I heard a great voice out of heaven saying, Behold, the tabernacle of God is with men."*—REVELATION xxi. 3.

> "How far from here to heaven?
>   Not very far, my friend;
>   A single hearty step
>   Will all thy journey end.—
> Hold there! where runnest thou?
>   Know, heaven is in thee!
> Seek'st thou for God elsewhere,
>   His face thou'lt never see."—*Silesius.*

"It makes no difference—whether we live or die, we are in the presence of God."—*George Eliot.*

---

17. *"Teach me thy way, O Lord; I will walk in thy truth: unite my heart to fear thy name."*—PSALM lxxxvi. 11.

> "O Holy Spirit, fount of breath,
>   Whose comforts never fail nor fade,
> Vouchsafe the life that knows no death,
>   Vouchsafe the light that knows no shade;
> And grant, that we through all our days
> May share thy gifts, and sing thy praise."

"After all, the most natural beauty in the world is honesty and moral truth; for all beauty is truth."—*Shaftesbury.*

---

18. *"Thus saith the Lord of hosts; consider your ways."*— HAGGAI i. 7.

> "As Christ hath loved us, grant us grace
>   Thine acceptable will to prove,
> In filial fear to seek thy face,
>   And as thy children walk in love."—
>   *Downton.*

"It is pleasant to see a notorious profligate seized with a concern for religion, and converting his spleen into zeal."—*Addison.*

19. *" The Lord will not forsake his people, for his great name's sake."*—I SAMUEL xii. 22.

> " Let us his faithfulness proclaim,
> The keenest pangs He hath not sent,
> He mercy blends with chastisement;
> And hot though be his anger's flame,
> Yet is his rod a father's rod,
> And He is still compassion's God."—
>
> *From the Dutch.*

" Did God ever leave his children to want? He gives their food to the little ones of the birds, and his goodness extends over all nature."—*Racine.*

---

20. *" Turn ye unto Me, saith the Lord of Hosts, and I will turn unto you."*—ZECHARIAH i. 3.

> " Omnipotence is on your side,
> And Wisdom watches o'er your heads,
> And God Himself will be your guide,
> So ye but follow where He leads."—
>
> *Lehr.*

" The call to religion is not a call to be better than your fellows, but to be better than yourself."—*Beecher.*

---

21. *" Above all things have fervent charity among yourselves."*—I PETER iv. 8.

> " Oh, help each other, hasten on,
> Behold the goal is nigh at hand;
> The battle-field shall soon be won,
> Your King before you soon shall stand."

Charity is—" Gently to hear, kindly to judge."—*Shakespere.*

G

22. *"A merry heart maketh a cheerful countenance.—A merry heart doeth good like a medicine."*—PROVERBS xv. 13. xvii. 22.

> "A thought of joy, that comes with sudden power,
> When least the welcome guest we look'd to find.
> Who sends that thought? whence springs it?
> Like the wind,
> Its passage is invisible."—
> > *C. Campbell.*

"Joy is one of the greatest panaceas of life."—*Hukeland.*

23. *"The Lord is our judge, the Lord is our lawgiver, the Lord is our king; He will save us."*—ISAIAH xxxiii. 22.

> "In darkest shades if He appear,
> My dawning is begun;
> He is my soul's sweet morning-star,
> And He my rising sun."—
> > *Watts.*

"Laws, written, if not on stone tables, yet on the azure of infinitude, in the inner heart of God's creation, certain as life, certain as death! I say, the laws are there, and thou shalt not disobey them."—*Carlyle.*

24. *"Whosoever doeth not righteousness is not of God, neither he that loveth not his brother."*—I JOHN iii. 10.

> "Lord I have inly found Thee,
> Depart Thou not from me,
> But wrap thy love around me,
> And keep me close to Thee."—
> > *Novalis.*

"The Christian that seeks to reach heaven by Christ the way, will not only feel all the safety of his course, but he will be characterised, whilst he walks it, by whatsoever things are pure, whatsoever things are just, and lovely, and of good report."—*Dr. Cumming.*

25. *"I will give unto him that is athirst of the fountain of the water of life freely."*—REVELATION xxi. 6.

> " What thanks I owe Thee, and what love,
>   A boundless, endless store,
> Shall echo through the realms above
>   When time shall be no more."—
>
> > *Cowper.*

" If thou desirest a noble and holy life, and unceasingly prayest to God for it, if thou continue constant in this thy desire, it will be granted unto thee without fail."—*St. Bernard.*

---

26. *"Shew me a token for good."*—PSALM lxxxvi. 17.

> " There's not a bird with lonely nest
>   In pathless wood or mountain crest,
> Nor meaner thing, which does not share,
>   O God ! in thy paternal care."—
>
> > *B. W. Noel.*

" There is religion in everything around us—a calm and holy religion in the unbreathing things of nature, which man would do well to imitate."—*Ruskin.*

---

27. *"And, without all contradiction, the less is blessed of the better."*—HEBREWS vii. 7.

> " Ye fearful saints, fresh courage take ;
>   The clouds ye so much dread
> Are big with mercy, and shall break
>   In blessings on your head."—
>
> > *Cowper.*

" A superior is never made for his own profit, but for the profit of the inferior."—*Montaigne.*

28. "*It is better, if the will of God be so, that ye suffer for well doing, than for evil doing.*"—1 PETER iii. 17.

> " His thoughts are high, his love is wise,
>   His wounds a cure intend ;
> And, though He does not always smile,
>   He loves unto the end."—
>   *Mason.*

" Virtue, though in rags, may challenge more than vice set off with all the trim of greatness."—*Massinger.*

---

29. "*I will teach you the good and the right way, only fear the Lord, and serve Him in truth with all your heart.*—1 SAMUEL xii. 23, 24.

> " Only that, dear, neither wise nor fair,
>   Just as commonplace as bread you eat,
> Or as water flowing everywhere,
>   Or the homely grass beneath your feet.
> Only faithful,—does the want alarm you ?
> Only faithful,—will the word not charm you ?"—
>   *Williams.*

" Truth is the ground of science, the centre wherein all things repose, and is the type of eternity."—*Sir. P. Sidney.*

---

30. "*The spirit of man is the candle of the Lord.*"—PROVERBS xx. 27.

> " He knows our souls in all their fears,
>   And gently wipes our falling tears ;
> Forms trembling voices to a song,
>   And bids the feeble heart be strong."—
>   *Doddridge.*

" Whatever that be which thinks, which understands, which wills, which acts, it is something celestial and divine; and, upon that account, must necessarily be eternal."—*Cicero.*

84

31. *"Abide in Him; that when He shall appear, we may have confidence, and not be ashamed before Him."*—I JOHN ii. 28.

> " The future still is hid with Thee,
>   Its secret Thou dost know :
> We cannot guess its coming bliss,
>   And we would have it so :
> Content, when this year's course is o'er,
> We shall but love and trust Thee more."—
>
> *I. Fyvie.*

" The faithful Christian will always find occasions in which he may testify his fidelity to Christ, by labouring to instruct the ignorant, and by administering assistance and comfort to his afflicted brethren."—*Mant.*

1. *"Seek ye out of the book of the Lord, and read."*—ISAIAH
xxxiv. 16.

> " Two ways we have by which to reach the height
> Of heaven's high grace : the one is to explore
> The sacred writings, from whose blessed lore
> Shines to the quickened eye the purest light ;
> The other is to raise the inward sight
> Up to the cross, and there, with reverend look,
> Peruse Himself."—*V. Colonna.*

It is a belief in the Bible, the fruits of deep meditation, which
has served me as the guide of my moral and literary life."—*Goethe.*

---

2. *" Worship God: for the testimony of Jesus is the spirit of
prophecy."*—REVELATION xix. 10.

> " Praise God ! upon the earth
> His praise is sounding ;
> On every ocean shore
> Voices of many waters are resounding
> His praise for evermore."—*I. Craig.*

" Feeling itself, like Enoch, walking with God, the heart perceives
a spirituality and purity in every joy, a mercy and a balm in every
sorrow."—*Matthew.*

---

3. *" Be ready always to give an answer to every man that asketh
you a reason of the hope that is in you with meekness and
fear : having a good conscience."*—I PETER iii. 15, 16.

> " What then, Christian, says thy faith ?
> Our Lord is Lord of hell and death.
> Child of created man ! He was as thou,
> That thou—as He—might victor be
> O'er all that brings decay on things below.
> Let His truth work."

" Hope is a vigorous principle ; it is furnished with light and heat
to advise and execute ; it sets the head and heart to work, and
animates a man to do his utmost."—*J. Collier.*

4. *" He that saith he abideth in Him ought himself also so to walk, even as He walked."*—I JOHN ii. 6.

" O Lord, the pilot's part perform,
　And guide and guard me through the storm ;
　Defend me from each threatening ill,
　Control the waves, say, ' Peace, be still.' "—

Cowper.

" Many there are who, while they bear the name of Christians, are totally unacquainted with the power of their divine religion. Christianity is with them a geographical, not a descriptive, appellation."—*Faber.*

---

5. *" His foundation is in the holy mountains."*—PSALM lxxxvii. 1.

" To Him, untrodden, snow-clad, star-crowned mountains
　　Life up their altars hoar,
　To Him, from far-off undiscovered fountains
　　Unsullied rivers pour."—

I. Craig.

" Nature is the chart of God."—*Tupper.*

---

6. *" The Lord seeth not as man seeth; for man looketh on the outward appearance, but the Lord looketh on the heart."*—I SAMUEL xvi. 7.

" For though, seduced and led astray,
　　Thou'st travelled far, and wandered long,
　Thy God hath seen thee all the way,
　　And all the turns that led thee wrong."

" Men are not to be judged by their looks, habits, and appearances ; but by the character of their lives and conversations, and by their works."—*Sir R. L'Estrange.*

87

7. *"To do justice and judgment is more acceptable to the Lord than sacrifice."*—PROVERBS xxi. 3.

" Though to human senses
Passionless and dumb,
How the life that now is
Talks of that to come."

" What is justice ?—To give every man his due."—*Aristotle.*

---

8. *"Behold, God is my salvation ; I will trust, and not be afraid: for the Lord Jehovah is my strength and my song."*— ISAIAH xii. 2.

" He is my Shepherd, I his sheep ;
I do not want to know
Whether the way be soft or steep
By which I am to go.
If green and smooth the mountain be,
I need not ask for more ;
If stony, He will carry me,
As He has done before."

" True religion is the foundation of society. When that is once shaken by contempt, the whole frabric cannot be stable nor lasting." —*Burke.*

---

9. *"Thus speaketh the Lord of hosts, saying, Execute true judgment, and shew mercy and compassions every man to his brother."*—ZECHARIAH vii. 9.

" Oh ! sweet the flow
Of grief that mourns an erring brother's woe :
But sweeter yet to see the warrior rude,
Iron of limb, and stern in mien and mood,
Bow to his God the strong but willing knce,
And drop the tear of meek humility."—*Kinglake.*

" Compassion is an emotion of which we ought never to be ashamed. Graceful, particularly in youth, is the tear of sympathy and the heart that melts at the tale of woe."—*Blair.*

10. "*The law made nothing perfect, but the bringing in of a better hope did; by the which we draw nigh unto God.*"—HEBREWS vii. 19.

> " Eternal God, what peace of mind has he,
> What light, what love, what joy of various kind,
> Whose heart, to sin and self no more inclined,
> With full desire is turned again to Thee !"—
>
> *V. Colonna.*

"Whatever enlarges hope, will also exalt courage."—*Johnson.*

11. "*O Lord God of hosts, who is a strong Lord like unto Thee?*"
—PSALM lxxxix. 8.

> " The spirit worn with straying
> Will find His judgment best :
> Oh, hear what He is saying,
> And yield thyself to rest."—
>
> *Waring.*

" God is eternity—God is truth—God is holiness. He has nothing, He is all, the whole heart conceives Him, but no thought.'
—*Richter.*

12. "*Comfort ye, comfort ye my people, saith your God.*"—ISAIAH xl. i.

> " In the hour of my distress,
> When temptations me oppress,
> And when I my sins confess,
> Sweet Spirit, comfort me."—
>
> *Herrick.*

" In the exhaustless catalogue of heaven's mercies to mankind, the power we have of finding some germs of comfort in the hardest trials must ever occupy the foremost place."—*Dickens.*

89

13. "*If we say that we have no sin, we deceive ourselves, and the truth is not in us.*"—1 JOHN i. 8.

"My soul, bear thou thy part,
    Triumph in God above,
And with a well-tuned heart
    Sing thou the songs of love !
Thou art His own whose precious blood,
Shed for thy good, His love made known."

"Sin is never at a stay : if we do not retreat from it, we shall advance in it ; and the further on we go, the more we have to come back."—*Barrow.*

14. "*Thou art righteous, O Lord, which art, and wast, and shalt be.*"—REVELATION xvi. 5.

"Lord, search my thoughts, and try my ways,
    And make my soul sincere ;
Then shall I stand before thy face,
    And find acceptance there."

"God never made his work for man to mend."—*Dryden.*

15. "*The Lord is not slack concerning his promise.*"—2 PETER iii. 9.

"Nor death nor life, nor earth nor hell,
    Nor time's destroying sway,
Can e'er efface us from his heart,
    Or make his love decay."—

"He gives to the flowers their beautiful tint ; He causes the fruits to grow and ripen ; He distributes to them in due proportion the warmth of the day and the coolness of the night ; the field which receives them gives them back with interest."—*Racine.*

16. "*Whoso stoppeth his ears at the cry of the poor, he also shall cry himself, but shall not be heard.*"—PROVERBS xxi. 13.

> "The poor are Thy peculiar care,
> To them Thy promises are sure :
> Thy gifts 'the poor in spirit' share ;
> Oh, may we ever thus be poor."

"None can be called deformed, but the unkind."—*Pope.*

---

17. "*The eyes of the Lord are over the righteous, and His ears are open unto their prayers.*"—1 PETER iii. 12.

> "Life's blessings free as water flow,
> From the same source divine ;
> Bid Jesus to the feast, and lo !
> He makes the water wine."

"Of what consequence is it that anything should be concealed from man ?—nothing is hidden from God : He is present in our minds and comes into the midst of our thoughts. Comes, do I say ?—as if He were ever absent !"—*Seneca.*

---

18. "*Let all things be done decently and in order.*"—1 CORINTHIANS xiv. 40.

> "Let us each be humble, fervent,
> Bloom to heaven, but root in earth,
> Show the Royal eyes observant,
> Homely, tender-hearted worth."

"Order is the sanity of the mind, the health of the body, the peace of the city, the security of the state."—*Southey.*

19. *"So teach us to number our days, that we may apply our hearts unto wisdom."*—PSALM xc. 12.

> "Graft me into Thee for ever,
>   Vine of life, that I may grow
> Stronger heavenward, drooping never,
>   For the sharpest storms that blow."—
>   *Dessler.*

"The sublimity of wisdom is to do those things living, which are to be desired when dying."—*Jeremy Taylor.*

---

20. *"The grass withereth, the flower fadeth; but the word of our God shall stand for ever."*—ISAIAH xl. 8.

> "When storms arise and seas of trouble roll,
>   I will be near to save the sinking soul ;
> Each wave that breaks shall lift, dilate your breast,
>   And in their motion—I will give you rest."—
>   *G. Massey.*

"God is simple and true in word and deed, never changes, never deceives any one by words."—*Plato.*

---

21. *"Consider Him that endured such contradiction of sinners against Himself, lest ye be wearied and faint in your minds."*—HEBREWS xii. 3.

> "O love so little losing ! at such cost
> Restoring to Thyself that little lost,
> This, this thy praise through worlds on worlds renown'd,
> 'Was dead, and is alive,—was lost, is found.'"—
>   *Monsell.*

"In the beautiful character of the blessed Jesus there was not a more striking feature than a certain sensibility, which disposed Him to take part in every one's affliction to which He was a witness."—*Bishop Horsley.*

92

22. *"And when even was come, the ship was in the midst of the sea, and He alone on the land."*—MARK vi. 47.

"Sweet is the close of day,
When all the fields are still;
Earth looks as if it listening lay
For God to speak his will."—

Knox.

"Evening is, also, the delight of virtuous age; it seems an emblem of the tranquil close of busy life—serene, placid, and mild, with the impress of its great Creator stamped upon it."—*Bulwer Lytton.*

---

23. *"He that will love life, and see good days, let him refrain his tongue from evil, and his lips that they speak no guile."*—I PETER iii. 10.

"For oh, how very dear is life!
How pleasant 'tis to live!
Of all the gifts His hands bestow,
He can no greater give."—

Horton.

"He lives long, that lives well; and time misspent is not lived, but lost."—*Fuller.*

---

24. *"With joy shall ye draw water out of the wells of salvation."*—ISAIAH xii. 3.

"If thou art poor—and poor thou art—
Lo, He has riches to impart;
Not wealth, in which mean avarice rolls,
Oh! better far, the wealth of souls."

"Joys are our wings, sorrows are our spurs."—*Richter.*

93

25. "*The Lord knoweth how to deliver the godly out of temptations.*"—2 PETER ii. 9.

> "Order all our way
> Through this mortal day ;
> In our toil with aid be near us ;
> In our need with succour cheer us ;
> When life's course is o'er,
> Open Thou the door."—
> *Russell.*

"Temptation is the fire that brings up the scum of the heart."—*Boston.*

26. "*My son, fear thou the Lord and the king : and meddle not with them that are given to change.*"—PROVERBS xxiv. 21.

> "When I was a youth,
> Not overrun by any care,
> In the peaceful path of truth
> Nightly did I hear this prayer—
> 'Jesus bless him.'"

"Character is a perfectly educated will."—*Novalis.*

27. "*Turn you to the Stronghold, ye prisoners of hope : even to-day do I declare that I will render double unto thee.*"—ZECHARIAH ix. 12.

> "Sister to Faith and Love ! sweet Grace,
> I woo thee to my breast ;
> O come, and with thy lovely face,
> Smile all my fears to rest."

"Hope is like the wing of an angel, soaring up to Heaven, and bearing our prayers to the throne of God."—*J. Taylor.*

28. "*Let the beauty of the Lord our God be upon us : and establish Thou the work of our hands upon us ; yea, the work of our hands establish Thou it.*"—PSALM xc. 17.

"Give strength, whene'er our strength must fail ;
    Give strength the flesh to curb ;
Give strength when craft and sin prevail
    To weaken and disturb.
        The world doth lay her snares
        To catch us unawares."—
                        Marperger.

"The greatest of all blessings, as it is the most ennobling of all privileges, is to be indeed a Christian."—*Coleridge.*

---

29.   "*Help Thou mine unbelief.*"—MARK ix. 24.

"Breathe on us, Lord, that we receive
    Fresh grace, to make our souls revive ;
    Bid the dry bones arise and live,—
        Good Spirit, hear and aid."—
                        Prichard.

"Prayer is a virtue that prevaileth against all temptations."—*Bernard.*

---

30. "*When the poor and needy seek water, and there is none, and their tongue faileth for thirst, I the Lord will hear them, I the God of Israel will not forsake them.*"—ISAIAH xli. 17.

"Come ye who struggle in a gulf of shame ;
    Come ye whose sin God only will forgive ;
    Come ! for I have for you a new white name :
        Arise and live."

"The Divinity is so great, and of such a character, that He both sees and hears all things, is everywhere present, and attends to all things."—*Xenophon.*

1. "*Continue thou in the things which thou hast learned and hast been assured of.*"—2 TIMOTHY iii. 14.

"My own dim life should teach me this,
That life shall live for evermore,
Else earth is darkness at the core,
And dust and ashes all that is."—
Tennyson.

"If you seriously resolve to be energetic and industrious, depend upon it you will for your whole life have reason to rejoice that you were wise enough to form and act upon that determination."—*Mrs. Buxton.*

2. "*Prove all things; hold fast that which is good.*"— 1 THESSALONIANS v. 21.

"All works are good, and each is best
As most it pleases Thee ;
Each worker pleases when the rest
He serves in charity :
And neither man nor work unblest
Wilt Thou permit to be."—
Lynch.

"Nothing must make a man's conscience a servant."—*Cromwell.*

3. "*A double-minded man is unstable in all his ways.*"— JAMES i. 8.

"Spurn not the call to life and light ;
Regard in time the warning kind ;
That call thou mayst not always slight,
And yet the gate of mercy find."—
Hyde.

"That which is won ill, will never wear well, for there is a curse attends it, which will waste it."—*Matthew Henry.*

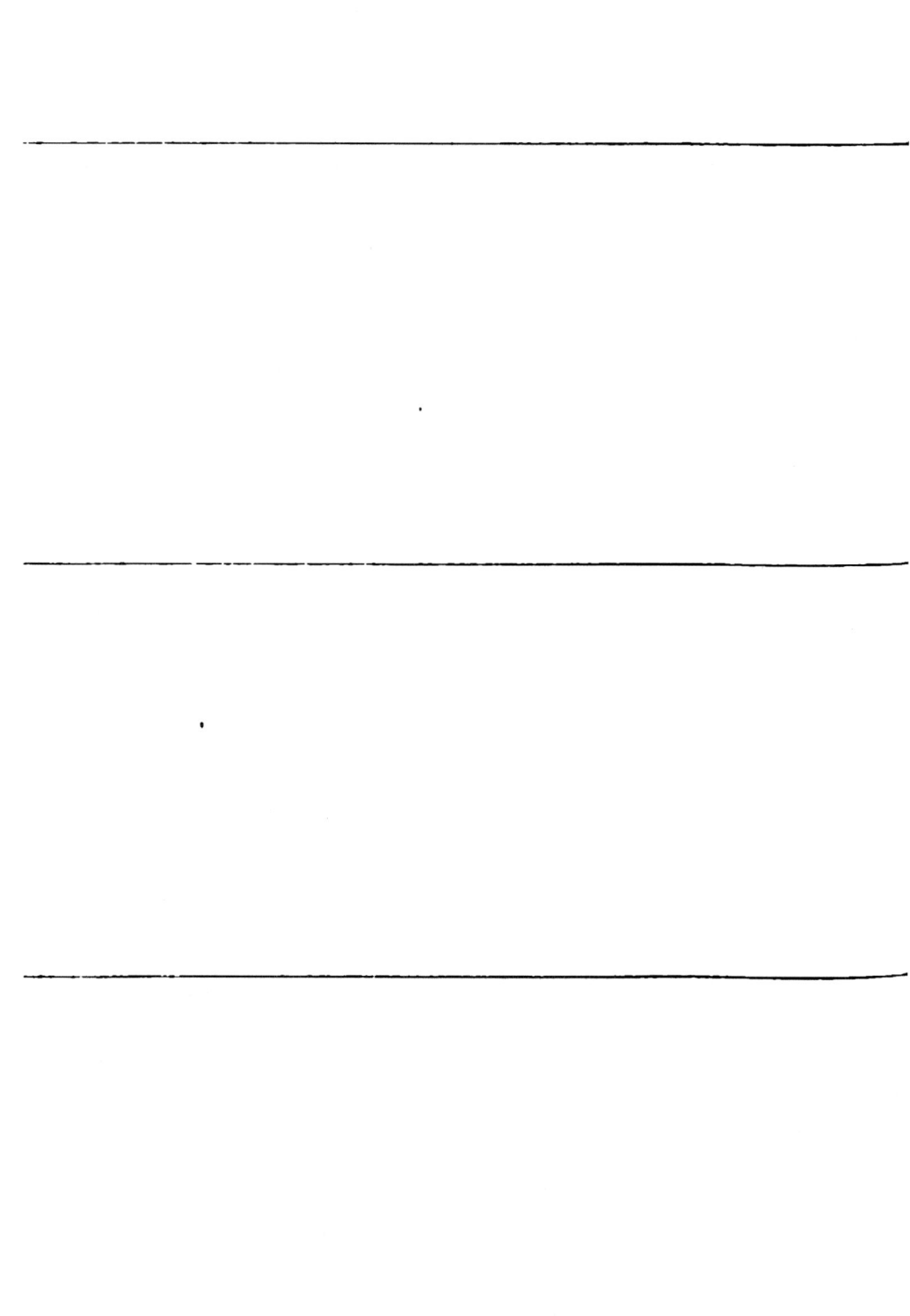

4. "*Godliness with contentment is great gain.*"—I TIMOTHY vi. 6.

> " Do thou then breathe such thoughts into my mind
> By which such virtue may in me be bred,
> That in Thy holy footsteps I may tread."—
>
> *M. Angelo.*

" Let no one think that it is hard to attain thereunto. Although it sounds hard, and is hard at first, yet, when one has reached this state, no life can be easier or sweeter, or fuller of pleasures."—*Tauler.*

5. "*Debate thy cause with thy neighbour himself; and discover not a secret to another.*"—PROVERBS xxv. 9.

> " 'Tis in my memory locked,
> And you yourself shall keep the key of it."—
>
> *Shakspere.*

" Free and fair discussion will ever be found the firmest friend to truth."—*G. Campbell.*

6. "*O remember not against us former iniquities; let Thy tender mercies speedily prevent us.*"—PSALM lxxix. 8.

> " Lead us to holiness,—the road,
> The narrow road which leads to God ;
> Lead us to Christ the living Way,
> Nor let us from His precepts stray."—
>
> *Browne.*

" Though the heart once gone from God turn continually away from Him, and move not toward Him till it be renewed, yet, even in its wandering, it retains that natural relation to God, as its centre, that it hath no true rest elsewhere, nor can by any means find it."—*Coleridge.*

7. " *Wisdom is justified of her children.*"—MATTHEW xi. 19.

> " Let us while here we dwell,
>   This one thought ponder well,
> That in God's likeness we are made.
>   As o'er a fruitful land
>   Rich harvests waving stand,
> We, serving Him, bear fruits that never fade."—
>
> *Schmolck.*

" In daily life, what distinguishes the master is the using those materials he has, instead of looking about for what are more renowned."—*Emerson.*

8. " *Consider what I say ; and the Lord give thee understanding in all things.*"—2 TIMOTHY ii. 7.

> " There is a book who runs may read,
>   Which heavenly truth imparts ;
> And all the lore its scholars need,
>   Pure eyes and Christian hearts."—
>
> *Keble.*

" To some men the mere fact of existence, the simple walking through the air and light, gives more pleasure than others find in the whole round of so-called life."—*Beecher.*

9. " *Where is boasting then ? It is excluded. By what law ? Of works ? Nay : but by the law of faith.*"—ROMANS iii. 27.

> " Know, the first step in Christian lore
>   Is to depart from sin ;
> True faith will leave the world no more
>   A place thy heart within."

" The empty vessel makes the greatest sound."—*Shakspere.*

10. "*Though I have the gift of prophecy, and understand all mysteries, and all knowledge; and though I have all faith, so that I could remove mountains, and have not charity, I am nothing.*"—I CORINTHIANS xiii. 2.

> "Oh, bind thyself with silver ties
> To men,—to God with golden bands!
> This is Religion; thus shall rise
> The house not made with hands."

"Men who concentrate themselves all upon one point, may be sharp, acute, pungent—they may have the spear-head force of character, but they are never broad and round, never of full-proportioned manhood."—*Beecher.*

11. "*He is able to succour them that are tempted.*"—HEBREWS ii. 18.

> "Thou, O Elder Brother! who
> In Thy flesh our trials knew,
> Thou who hast been touch'd by these
> Our most sad infirmities—
> Change the dream of me and mine,
> For the truth of Thee and Thine,
> And through chaos, doubt, and strife,
> Interpose Thy calm of life!"—*Whittier.*

"Here you can sit at the very feet of One who knows you wholly, who has been tried through sorrow and desertion and all forms of human suffering, and who can and does feel for you and with you in every secret struggle and every spiritual aspiration."

12. "*If any man among you seem to be religious, and bridleth not his tongue, but deceiveth his own heart, this man's religion is vain.*"— JAMES i. 26.

> "In what the world calls weakness lurks
> The very strength of evil,
> Still mighily it helps the works,
> Of our great foe the devil."

"Religion is the best thing, and the corruption of it the worst."—*Robinson.*

13. "*O, Timothy, keep that which is committed to thy trust, avoiding profane and vain babblings and oppositions of science falsely so called.*"—1 TIMOTHY vi. 20.

> "Then bless thy secret growth, nor catch
> At noise, but thrive unseen and dumb ;
> Keep clean, bear fruit, earn life, and watch
> Till the white-winged reapers come."—
> *H. Vaughan.*

"God does not cease to speak, but the noise of the creatures without, and of our passions within, confuses us, and prevents our hearing."—*Fénelon.*

14. "*Thy way is in the sea, and Thy path in the great waters, and Thy footsteps are not known.*"—PSALM lxxvii. 19.

> "Were I, O God, in churchless lands remaining,
> Far from all voice of teachers and divines,
> My soul would find in flowers of thy ordaining
> Priests, sermons, shrines."—*Horace Smith.*

"What does not the firmament alone preach to us—the clear blue heaven, or the same heaven covered with storm-clouds ! But how many hear ?"—*Tholuck.*

15. "*If we believe not, yet He abideth faithful.*"—
2 TIMOTHY ii. 13.

> "Why bursts such melody from tree and bush ;
> The overflowing of each songster's heart,
> So filling mine, that it can scarcely hush
> Awhile to listen, but would take its part ?
> 'Tis but one song I hear where'er I rove,
> Though countless be the notes, that God is love."—
> *T. Davis.*

"He is that divine principle which speaketh in our hearts, and without which there can be neither just apprehension nor rectitude of judgment."—*Thomas à Kempis.*

16. *" He that soweth the good seed is the Son of man; the field is the world."*—MATTHEW xiii. 37, 38.

" Thou art the Way ; by Thee alone
From sin and death we flee ;
And he who would the Father seek
Must seek Him, Lord, by Thee."—
Donne.

" Our present life in Him may be compared to that of a seed ; a hidden life, contending underground against cold and darkness and obstructions, yet bearing within its breast the indestructible germ of vitality."—

17. *" There are diversities of operations, but it is the same God which worketh all in all."*—1 CORINTHIANS xii. 6.

" Without thy presence, wealth is bags of cares ;
Wisdom, but folly ; joy, disquiet—sadness ;
Friendship is treason, and delights are snares ;
Pleasures but pain, and mirth but pleasing madness ;
Without Thee, Lord, things be not what they be."—
Quarles.

" He that hath not all Christian graces in their measure hath none ; and he that hath any one truly, hath all."—*Robinson.*

18. *" Who is he that will harm you, if ye be followers of that which is good ?"*—1 PETER iii. 13.

" Quiet in God,—the ever-present seal
Of faith unspoken,
Believing faces, infant lips, reveal
Its nameless token."

" I was early convinced that true religion consists in an inward life, wherein the heart doth love and reverence God the Creator, and doth learn to exercise true justice and goodness, not only toward all men, but also toward the brute creatures."—*Woolman.*

19. *"Seest thou a man that is hasty in his words? there is more hope of a fool than of him."*—PROVERBS xxix. 20.

"Every word has its own spirit,
　　True or false, that never dies ;
Every word man's lips have uttered
　　Echoes in God's skies."—

A. A. Proctor.

"Haste and rashness are storms and tempests, breaking and wrecking business."—*Fuller.*

---

20. *"Charge them that are rich in this world, that they be not high-minded, nor trust in uncertain riches."*—1 TIMOTHY vi. 17.

"By the thorn road, and no other,
　　Is the mount of triumph won :
Tread it without shrinking, brother ;
　　Jesus trod it : press thou on !"

"If you do not use the tools, they use you."—*Emerson.*

---

21. *"Mercy unto you, and peace, and love, be multiplied."*—JUDE 2.

"In the heart's depths, a peace serene and holy
　　Abides, and when pain seems to have her will,
Or we despair—O may that peace rise slowly,
　　Stronger than agony, and we be still."—

S. Johnson.

"Suffering rightly borne weakens that part in us that should be weak, and strengthens what should be strong."—*Beecher.*

22. *" Unto you that fear my name shall the Sun of Righteousness arise with healing in his wings."*—MALACHI iv. 2.

> " The light of Truth to us display,
> And make us know and love Thy way ;
> Plant holy fear in every heart,
> That we from Thee may ne'er depart."—
>
> *Browne.*

" Then not only will the stars shed upon us light, but they will pour from heaven sublimity into our minds, and from on high will rain down thoughts to make us noble."—*Euthanasy.*

23. *" The servant of the Lord must not strive; but be gentle unto all men, apt to teach, patient."*—2 TIMOTHY ii. 24.

> " O hearts of love ! O souls that turn
> Like sunflowers to the pure and best,
> To you the truth is manifest !
> For they the mind of Christ discern
> Who lean, like John, upon His breast."—
>
> *Whittier.*

" Modesty in your discourse will give a lustre to truth, and an excuse to your error."

24. *" As is the earthy, such are they also that are earthy : and as is the heavenly, such are they also that are heavenly."*—I CORINTHIANS xv. 48.

> " The way the holy prophets went,
> The way that leads from banishment,
> The king's highway of holiness,
> I'll go ; for all the paths are peace."—
>
> *Cennick.*

" Christ did not lead such a life as His for the sake of reward, but out of love ; and love maketh such a life light, and taketh away all its hardships."

25. *" Thou shalt increase my greatness and comfort me on every side."*—PSALM lxxi. 21.

> " Dear Comforter ! Eternal Love !
> If Thou wilt stay with me,
> Of lowly thoughts and simple ways,
> I'll build a house for Thee."—
>
> *Faber.*

" Nothing is more beautiful in the world of morals than the great man in talents who is the little child in religion."— *J. J. Gurney.*

---

26. *" Every creature of God is good, and nothing to be refused, if it be received with thanksgiving."*—1 TIMOTHY iv. 4.

> " Thou who hast given us eyes to see
> And love these sights so fair,
> Give us a heart to find out Thee,
> And view Thee everywhere."—
>
> *Keble.*

" A truly good and wise man should admire everything, or rather that infiniteness of wisdom and omnipotence which shows itself in every visible object."—*Bishop Hall.*

---

27. *" The word of the Lord endureth for ever. And this is the word which by the gospel is preached unto you."*— 1 PETER i. 25.

> " These, these, prepare us for the sight
> Of majesty above.
> The sons of ignorance and night,
> May dwell in the Eternal Light
> Through the Eternal Love."

" We must never forget that not only immortality, but *Life*, has been brought to light by the gospel."—*Grunwell.*

OCTOBER.

28.   "*The Lord God liveth.*"—JEREMIAH xlv. 26.

"O glory that no eye may bear !
O presence bright, our inner Guest !
O farthest off ! O ever near !
Most hidden and most manifest."

"Blessing us in countless forms and ways, or withholding such gifts of His bounty only the more truly to draw our hearts to Him, only to crown us with a yet more enduring lovingkindness, and a yet more tender mercy."

---

29.   "*Watch ye, stand fast in the faith, quit you like men, be strong.*"—1 CORINTHIANS xvi. 13.

"'Is this the way, my Father?' 'Tis my child,
Thou must pass through the tangled dreary wild,
If thou would'st reach the city undefiled,
Thy peaceful home above."

"It is a sure token of an hireling that he wisheth his work were at an end. But he who truly loveth it is not offended at its toil, nor suffering."

---

30.   "*O God, be not far from me.*"—PSALM lxxi. 12.

"Be near me when my light is low,
When the blood creeps, and the nerves prick
And tingle ; and the heart is sick,
And all the wheels of Being slow."—

Tennyson.

"There should, indeed, be a progress in our spiritual life : else that life will too plainly be giving way before the manifold influences which try to check and destroy it."—*Hare.*

31. *"God hath not given us the spirit of fear; but of power, and of love, and of a sound mind."*—2 TIMOTHY i. 7.

> " When the soul to sin hath died,
>   True and beautiful and sound,
> Then all earth is sanctified ;
>   Up springs paradise around."—
>
> *Emerson.*

" If my soul is to perceive God, it must be heavenly.   It is not of God's severity that He requires much from man ; it is of His great kindness that He will have the soul to open herself wider, to be able to receive much, that He may bestow much upon it."—*Tauler.*

NOVEMBER.

1. "*The Lord lift up his countenance upon thee, and give thee peace.*"—NUMBERS vi. 26.

> "Thou on the Lord rely ;
> So safe shalt thou go on ;
> Fix on His work thy steadfast eye,
> So shall thy work be done."—
>
> *Gerhardt.*

"Do the best you can where'er you are ; and, when that is accomplished, God will open a door for you."—*Beecher.*

2. "*Honour all men. Love the brotherhood. Fear God. Honour the king.*"—1 PETER ii. 17.

> "God save the people and their houses all,
> The thriving, striving, and both great and small !
> And let us on Thy love with one voice call,
> When the sun rises, and the shadows fall."—
>
> *Lynch.*

"I knew a man in a certain religious exaltation, who 'thought it an honour to wash his own face.' He seemed to me more sane than those who hold themselves cheap."—*Emerson.*

3. "*Obey my voice, and I will be your God, and ye shall be my people : and walk ye in all the ways that I have commanded you, that it may be well unto you.*"—JEREMIAH vii. 23.

> "Blest be Thy love, dear Lord,
> That taught us this sweet way,
> Only to love Thee for Thyself,
> And for that love obey."—
>
> *J. Austin.*

"The problem is neither more nor less than to learn the way of God, and come into practical acquaintance with Him. And how can this be done without a large experience of defeat and disasters endlessly varied ?"—*Bushnell.*

4. "*O send out Thy light and Thy truth: let them lead me.*"—
PSALM xliii. 3.

"And what I am beheld again
What is, and no man understands;
And out of darkness came the hands
That reach thro' nature, moulding men."—
Tennyson.

"Apply to Him to open thine eyes, that thou mayst recognise his quiet and holy household."—*Krummacher.*

5. "*When I sit in darkness, the Lord shall be a light unto me.*"—
MICAH vii. 8.

"A ray
Upon this darkness suddenly may dart,
And Christ's dear love be poured into the heart,
To clothe creation in a robe of day.
Then doth the morning cheer, the night hath calm,
And skies a glory, and the dews a balm."

"In Him dawns a hope. Light breaks in, peace settles on the air; lo! the prison walls are giving way."—*Bushnell.*

6. "*His mercy is on them that fear Him, from generation to generation.*"—LUKE i. 50.

"Of what an easy quick access,
My blessed Lord, art Thou! how suddenly
May our requests Thine ear invade!
To show that state dislikes not easiness,
If I but lift mine eyes my suit is made;
Thou canst no more not hear, than Thou canst die."—
G. Herbert.

"They will come, the times of distress, in which our human neighbours have neither power nor will to help us. But along with them comes the Holy Spirit, whom the Saviour promised to send, and lifts up man's downcast eyes."—*Hossbach.*

7. *"Godly sorrow worketh repentance to salvation not to be repented of."*—2 CORINTHIANS vii. 10.

"O Thou who art our life,
   Be with us through the strife!
Thine own meek head was by earth's tempests bowed.
   Raise Thou our eyes above
   To see a Father's love,
Gleam, like the bow of promise, through the cloud!"—

Miles.

"The more difficulties one has to encounter, within and without, the more significant and the higher in inspiration his life will be."

---

8. *"Speak thou the things which become sound doctrine."*—TITUS ii. 1.

"Let me remeditate the truth
   That Christ did for and with us bleed,
Then, 'He is good that doeth good,'
   Shall be my dear and honoured creed."—

Lynch.

"In the Christian graces, humility stands highest of all, in the form of the Madonna; and in life, this is the secret of the wise."—*Emerson.*

---

9. *"Let patience have her perfect work."*—JAMES i. 4.

"Complain not that the way is long—what road is
   weary that leads there?
But let the angel take thy hand, and lead thee up
   the misty stair,
And then with beating heart await the opening of
   the Golden Gate."—

A. A. Proctor.

"It is most sweet that he who is not persuaded have patience towards them that are, and judge not."—*Cromwell.*

10. *"Call to remembrance the former days."*—HEBREWS x. 32.

"Dost thou remember all those happy meetings,
    In summer evenings round the open door ;
Kind looks, kind words, and tender greetings
    From clasping hands whose pulses beat no more.
Dost thou remember them ?"

"As in our moral, so in our spiritual life, no moment stands alone. There is no moment in it, which is not connected by indissoluble ties of motive and impulse with all that we have hitherto felt, and thought, and done."—*Hare.*

11. *"Many, O Lord God, are Thy wonderful works which Thou hast done, and Thy thoughts which are to us-ward: they cannot be reckoned up in order unto Thee."*—PSALM xl. 5.

"That we have lived, live now, and know we live,
And see Thy bounties from the heavens come down
With sunlight, moonlight, and the fruitful rain,
We praise Thee, praise Thee, Lord of light and life."—
                                      Freeland.

"We speak more truly than we are aware, when we say, as we often do, that we can form no idea of what heaven really is, until we arrive there."—*Greenwell.*

12. *"Unto the pure all things are pure : but unto them that are defiled and unbelieving is nothing pure."*—TITUS i. 15.

"Let me love Thee more and more,
    If I love at all, I pray ;
If I have not loved before,
    Help me to begin to-day."—
                                      Newton.

"Health, beauty, vigour, riches, and all the other things called goods, operate equally as evils to the vicious and unjust, as they do as benefits to the just."—*Plato.*

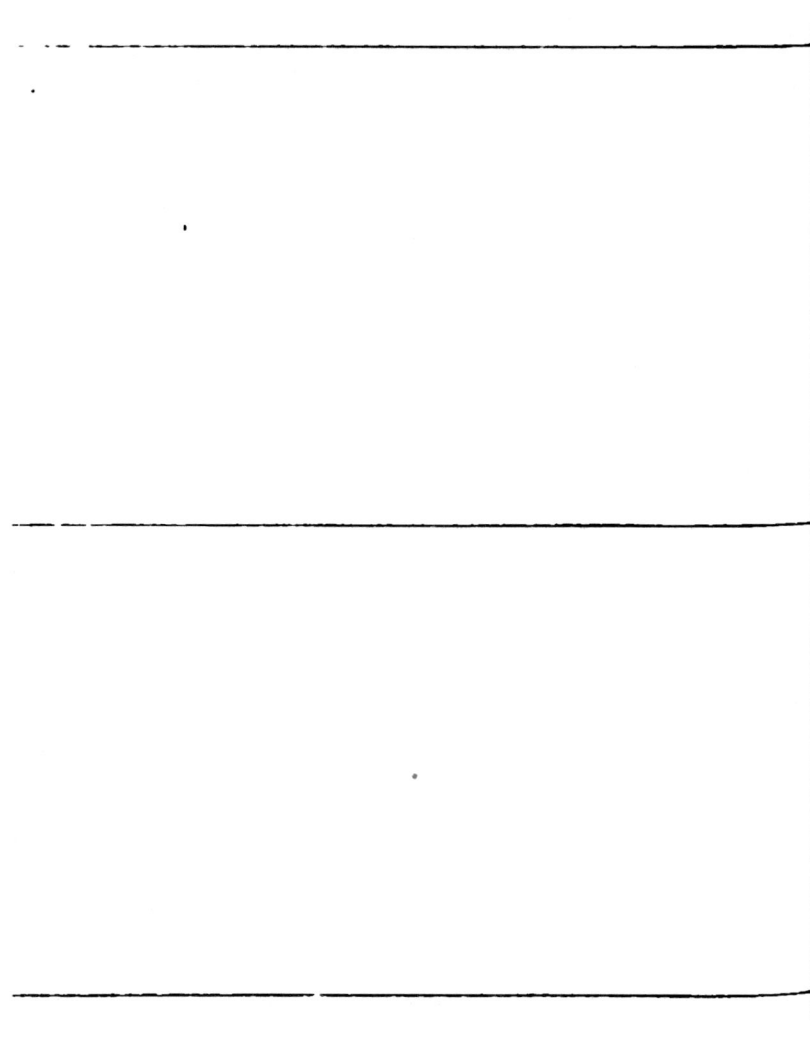

13. "*Thou, O Lord, art in the midst of us, and we are called by Thy name; leave us not.*"—JEREMIAH xvi. 9.

> "Who made this beating heart of mine
> But Thou, my heavenly Guest?
> Let no one have it then, but Thee;
> And let it be Thy rest!"—
>
> *Faber.*

"One of the most important and difficult things to realise in this life is that God is really with us (not against us) continually, watching the working of every human sympathy with the anxious interest of its Creator, and ever willing to direct and help."—*Gordon.*

14. "*He hath filled the hungry with good things.*"—LUKE i. 53.

> "O hope of every contrite heart!
> O joy of all the meek!
> To those who fall how kind Thou art!
> How good to those who seek!"—
>
> *St. Bernard.*

"For one great object of His divine mission was to renew the broken chain of love which once bound man to man, and become himself the centre link in the chain of humanity."—*Crombie.*

15. "*God is able to make all grace abound toward you.*"—2 CORINTHIANS ix. 8.

> "The dew of heaven is like Thy grace—
> It steals in silence down;
> But where it lights, the favoured place
> By richest fruit is known."—
>
> *Keble.*

"Therefore do not relinquish your desire, though it be not fulfilled immediately, or though ye may swerve from your aspirations, or even forget them for a time."—*Tauler.*

16. "*If any of you lack wisdom, let him ask of God, that giveth to all men liberally.*"—JAMES i. 5.

"Nor dare to blame God's gifts for incompleteness ;
  In that want their beauty lies : they roll
Towards some infinite depth of love and sweetness,
  Bearing onward man's reluctant soul."—

A. A. Proctor.

"And if God should not give it thee then, thou wilt find it in Him in eternity ; of this be assured."—*St. Bernard.*

17. "*He that cometh to God must believe that He is, and that He is a rewarder of them that diligently seek Him.*"—HEBREWS xi. 6.

"O break my heart ; but break it as the field
  Is by the plough upbroken for the corn :
O, break it as the buds, by green-leaf sealed,
  Are, to unloose the golden blossom, torn."—

Lynch.

"God will certainly take care of you, if you bear your whole weight on Him. He may not do it just in your way ; but He will do it."

18. "*I will look unto the Lord; I will wait for the God of my salvation : my God will hear me.*"—MICAH vii. 7.

"So long Thy power has blessed me ; sure it still
    Will lead me on,
O'er moor and fen, o'er crag and torrent, till
    The night is gone."—*J. H. Newman.*

"Is religion then a fantasy, when it can so uphold the soul amid all the waves of trouble? I tell you, *No.* I tell you it is *a very comfortable thing* to find refuge from every distressful care in the love of God."

Beecher.

19. *"Love the truth and peace."*—ZECHARIAH viii. 19.

> "O refresh us with Thy blessing,
>   O refresh us with Thy grace ;
> May Thy mercies, never ceasing,
>   Fit us for Thy dwelling-place !"—
>
> *Hastings.*

"Truth will never corrode ; it has sometimes a dull appearance, but that is because it is solid metal, just as the most placid-looking waters are the deepest."—*Burnett.*

20. *Jesus said—"Go ye and learn what that meaneth, I will have mercy, and not sacrifice."*—MATTHEW ix. 13.

> "And judge none lost ; but wait, and see,
>   With hopeful pity, not disdain ;
> The depth of the abyss may be
>   The measure of the height of pain
> And love and glory that may raise
>   This soul to God in after days !"—
>
> *A. A. Proctor.*

"Since the generality of persons act from impulse, much more than from principle, men are neither so good nor so bad as we are apt to think them."—*Hare.*

21. *"Exact no more than that which is appointed you."*— LUKE iii. 13.

> "Of mortal justice if thou scorn the rod,
>   Believe and tremble, thou art judged of God."—
>
> *Swenam.*

"A tyrant never tasteth of true friendship, nor of perfect liberty."—*Diogenes.*

22. *"If there be first a willing mind, it is accepted according to that a man hath, and not according to that he hath not."*— 2 CORINTHIANS viii. 12.

> "Who willing service gives,
>   Alone is truly free ;
> He finds the law by which he lives,
>   A law of liberty."

" What we can DO is a small thing ; but we can will and aspire to great things.   Thus if a man cannot be great, he can be good in will."—*Tauler.*

---

23. *"Like as a father pitieth his children, so the Lord pitieth them that fear Him."*—PSALM ciii. 13.

> " The crown must be won for heaven, my dear,
>   In the battle-field of life :
> My child, though thy foes are strong and tried,
>   He loveth the weak and small ;
> The angels of heaven are on thy side,
>   And God is over all."—
>   *A. A. Proctor.*

" Cannot a God so good charm you ?"—*Racine.*

---

24. *"A bishop must be blameless, as the steward of God : a lover of hospitality, a lover of good men, sober, just, holy, temperate."*—TITUS i. 7, 8.

> " The sacred word, so fraught with use,
>   Is bright with beauty too,
> Oft startling us like blooms profuse
>   Upon a sudden view."—
>   *Lynch.*

" Oh, where are those noble souls to be found, who, all unconscious of themselves, daily pursue their career like the sun ?"—*Tholuck.*

25. *"If ye endure chastening, God dealeth with you as with sons; for what son is he whom the father chasteneth not?"*—HEBREWS xii. 7.

> " Like a dream all my toil will vanish,
>   When I lay my head on His breast ;
> But the journey is very weary,
>   And He only can give me rest !"—
>
> *A. A. Proctor.*

" All the conditions of our life are raised thus, by the meaning He has shown to be in them, and the grace He has put upon them."—*Bushnell.*

26. *"It is an honour for a man to cease from strife: but every fool will be meddling."*—PROVERBS xx. 3.

> " Peace hath her victories,
>   No less renown'd than war."—
>
> *Milton.*

" People have no right to make fools of themselves, unless they have no relations to blush for them."—*Haliburton.*

27. *"Ye shall not afflict any widow or fatherless child."*—EXODUS xxii. 22.

> " The man who wears injustice by his side
>   Though powerful millions followed him to war,
> Combats against the odds—against high heaven."—
>
> *Havard.*

" Neither may a man who is made partaker of the divine nature, oppress or grieve any one. That is, it never entereth into his thoughts, to cause pain or distress to any, either by deed or neglect, by speech or silence."

28. *" The Lord our God be with us, as He was with our fathers."*
—1 KINGS viii. 57.

" With piety the young men bless,
  And through the nation shed abroad
  True virtue and the fear of God,
  A nation's happiness."—

Gerhardt.

And give us, " The joy of knowing that nothing can ever pluck
us out of His hand ; and that whatever may happen His goodness
towards us remains eternally the same."—*Dr. Vinet.*

---

29. *" They were astonished at his doctrine : for his word was
with power."*—LUKE iv. 32.

" God's help is always sure,
  His method's seldom guessed ;
  Delay will make our pleasure pure,
  Surprise will give it zest."—

Lynch.

" Nothing astonishes people more in this world than when a man
stands up calmly and tells the truth without respect of persons."—
Burnett.

---

30. *" Providing for honest things, not only in the sight of the
Lord, but also in the sight of men."*—2 CORINTHIANS viii. 21.

" On Thee is all this world upstaid,
  And in Thy hands doth rest ;
  And Thou canst wayward hearts persuade
  To turn as seems Thee best."

" Without doubt there be many men who are ensamples of virtue
and propriety on the Lord's Day, and pillars of his church here, who
are by no means beloved of their clerks at the shop, and that without fault on the clerks' side."—*S. Gordon.*

DECEMBER.

1. *"What a Word is this ! for with authority and power He commandeth the unclean spirits, and they come out."*—LUKE iv. 36.

> "Say not, my soul, 'From whence
> Can God relieve my care?'
> Remember that Omnipotence
> Has servants everywhere."—
>
> *Lynch.*

"Thou hast at this moment a very faint idea of the glory to which thy Redeemer has raised thee, or the completeness with which He has enriched thee."—*Spurgeon.*

2. *"Study to show thyself approved unto God, a workman that needeth not to be ashamed."*—2 TIMOTHY ii. 15.

> "Art Thou not evermore the same?
> And hast Thou not revealed
> That Thou wilt ever be our strength, Thy name
> Our tower of hope, our shield?"

"A man's true greatness lies in the consciousness of an honest purpose in life, founded on a just estimate of himself and every-thing else, on frequent self-examination, and a steady obedience to the rule which he knows to be right."—*Long.*

3. *"Comfort yourselves together, and edify one another."*—I THESSALONIANS v. 11.

> "I know that I am in Thy hands,
> Whose thoughts are peace toward me,
> That ever sure Thy counsel stands,
> Could I but build on Thee!"

"Sorrow sobers us, and makes the mind genial. And in sorrow we love and trust our friends more tenderly."—*Euthanasy.*

4. *"Beware lest any man spoil you through philosophy and vain deceit, after the tradition of men."*—COLOSSIANS ii. 8.

"To thee, to all, my sinking voice,
    Beloved, would once more proclaim,
In Christ alone mayst thou rejoice,
    Deceived by every other name."—

Sterling.

" I know where to *have* a man that hath principles."—*Cromwell.*

5. *"Paul said, I can do all things through Christ which strengtheneth me."*—PHILIPPIANS iv. 13.

" In having all things, and not Thee, what have I ?
Not having Thee, what have my labours got ?
Let me enjoy but Thee, what further crave I ?
And having Thee alone, what have I not ?"—

Quarles.

" However the world may affect to despise the genuine Christian, it is beyond their power ; they feel too sensibly the necessity of attaining that very state of feeling and disposition which is displayed in such a character."—*Wolfe.*

6. *"Stand therefore, having your loins girt about with truth, and having on the breastplate of righteousness."*—EPHESIANS vi. 14.

" Sure I must fight, if I would reign ;
    Increase my courage, Lord !
I'll bear the toil, endure the pain,
    Supported by Thy word."—

" Truth is the hiest thing that man may kepe."—*Chaucer.*

7. *"O give thanks unto the Lord, for He is good; for his mercy endureth for ever."*—PSALM cvii. 1.

> " A sure stronghold our God is He,
> A trusty shield and weapon ;
> Our help He'll be and set us free
> From every ill can happen."—
>
> *Luther.*

" Only he who in his heart is conscious of the grace of God perceives that the world also is full of the wonders of His grace."

---

8. *"The earth is the Lord's, and the fullness thereof."*— 1 CORINTHIANS x. 26.

> " The smallest moss upon a stone,
> Like 'writing on the wall,'
> Can only be explained by One,
> Though known and read of all."—
>
> *Macmillan.*

" The voice with which nature speaks to man is as the glance of a friend, and as the pressure of the hand, which are understood by all nations without speaking."—*Tholuck.*

---

9. *" Every word of God is pure: He is a shield unto them that put their trust in Him."*—PROVERBS xxx. 5.

> " And when the gleams of day retire,
> And midnight spreads its dark control,
> Love's secret whispers still inspire
> Their holy lessons in the soul."—
>
> *Madame Guyon.*

" The fewness of God's words, the magnitude of his actions, the fulness of his promises, and the unmistakable reality of his help, are facts that the feeblest Christian can advocate and the acutest infidel cannot shake."—*Burnett.*

10. *"A man's wisdom maketh his face to shine."*—
ECCLESIASTES viii. I.

"My blessed Lord! what bliss to feel Thee near,
 Faithful and true ;
To trust in Thee, without one doubt or fear,
 Thy will to do ;
And all the while to know that Thou, our friend,
Art blessing us, and wilt bless to the end."—

          Bateman.

"The mind is the man. If that be kept pure, a man signifies somewhat ; if not, I would very fain see what difference there is betwixt him and a beast. He hath only some activity to do some more mischief."—*Cromwell.*

11. *"My presence shall go with thee, and I will give thee rest."*—
EXODUS xxxiii. 14.

"As light and warmth to noontide hours,
 To sweetest voices tuneful songs,
And as to summer fields the flowers,
 So heaven to heavenly souls belongs."—

          Sterling.

"Where hast thou not walked with me, O Truth! teaching me what to beware, and what to desire?"—*St. Augustine.*

12. *"Every man shall bear his own burden."*—GALATIANS vi. 5.

"Dwells within the soul of every artist
 More than all his effort can express ;
And he knows the best remains unuttered ;
 Sighing at what *we* call his success."—

          A. A. Proctor.

"If a man take not his own burden well, he shall hardly understand others."

13. *"Remember me, O Lord, with the favour that Thou bearest unto Thy people."*—PSALM cvi. 4.

> " Nor mine the sweetness or the skill,
> But mine the love that will not tire,
> And, born of love, the vague desire
> That spurs the imitative will."—
>
> *Tennyson.*

" Christianity is, being like-minded with Christ ; it is considering Him as our sanctification as well as our redemption ; it is endeavouring to live to Him here, that we may live with Him hereafter."— *Hannah More.*

14. *"There is a generation, O how lofty are their eyes! and their eyelids are lifted up."*—PROVERBS xxx. 13.

> " O, were this but understood,
> To be great we must be good ;
> Learning then of Christ, we should
> Humbly serve and wait."—
>
> *Lynch.*

" As thou desirest the love of God and man, beware of pride : it is a tumour in thy mind, that breaks and poisons all thy actions."— *Quarles.*

15. *"Consecrate yourselves to-day to the Lord."*—EXODUS xxxii. 29.

> " Shall I see the fair sun waking,
> And not feel it wakes for me ?
> Each glad morning brightly breaking,
> And not feel it breaks for me ?"—
>
> *Bonar.*

" Either take Christ in your lives, or cast Him out of your lips ; either be that thou seemest, or else be what thou art."—*Dyer.*

16. "*Hearken unto Me, ye that know righteousness, the people in whose heart is my law; fear ye not the reproach of men, neither be ye afraid of their revilings.*"—ISAIAH li. 7.

"All my life I still have found,
　And I will forget it never,
Every sorrow hath its bound,
　And no cross endures for ever."

"Without constancy there is neither love, friendship, nor virtue in the world."—*Addison.*

---

17. "*They that sow in tears shall reap in joy.*"—PSALM cxxvi. 5.

"Yet less of sorrow lives in me
　For days of happy commune dead ;
　Less yearning for the friendship fled,
Than for some strong bond which is to be."—

Tennyson.

"We are as sure of trouble in this world as of waves on the sea : but while the waves toss, we travel."—*Lynch.*

---

18. "*There are . . . . . so many kinds of voices in the world, and none of them is without signification.*"—1 CORINTHIANS xiv. 10.

"Everywhere about us are they glowing,
　Some, like stars, to tell us spring is born ;
Others, their blue eyes with tears o'erflowing,
　Stand, like Ruth, amid the golden corn."

"When we contemplate the wonderful works of Nature, and, walking about at leisure, gaze upon this ample theatre of the world, considering the stately beauty, constant order, and sumptuous furniture thereof,—then should our hearts be affected with thankful sense, and our lips break forth in praise."—*Barrow.*

DECEMBER.

---

19. *"As a bird that wandereth from her nest, so is a man that wandereth from his place."*—PROVERBS xxvii. 8.

"Oft from Thy royal road we part,
Lost in the mazes of the heart :
Our lamps put out, our course forgot,
We seek for God and find Him not."—

Palgrave.

"Indecision is that slatternly housewife by whose fault chiefly the moth and the rust are allowed to make such dull work of life."—*E. Clarel.*

---

20. *"There is not a just man upon earth that doeth good and sinneth not."*—ECCLESIASTES vii. 20.

"We look up in our littleness
To Thy majestic state ;
Our comfort is Thou art so good,
And that Thou art so great."—

Faber.

"He that falls into sin is a man; that grieves at it may be a saint; that boasteth of it may be a devil."—*Fuller.*

---

21. *"I the Lord love judgment, I hate robbery for burnt offering."*—ISAIAH lxi. 8.

"O worship the Lord in the beauty of holiness !
Bow down before Him, His glory proclaim,
With gold of obedience, and incense of lowliness,
Kneel and adore Him, the Lord is His name."—

Monsell.

"Truly, that is no common thing to which our Lord refers, when He speaks of doing good ; the left hand not knowing what the right hand does ; the witness being that Eye only which seeth in secret."—*Tholuck.*

253

22. *"Do good, O Lord, unto those that be good, and to them that are upright in their hearts."*—PSALM cxxv. 4.

"Lord, we Thy presence seek ;
May ours this blessing be ;
Give us a pure and lowly heart,
A temple meet for Thee."—
Keble.

"It is not enough to know the outward facts of a man's life in order to know him.   His actions are the smallest part of him."—*Clarke.*

23. *"Let not thine heart envy sinners : but be thou in the fear of the Lord all the day long.   For surely there is an end."*—PROVERBS xxiii. 17. 18.

"When to laborious duties called,
Or by temptation tried,   ·
We'll seek the shelter of Thy wings,
And in Thy strength confide."—
Doddridge.

"Were the visage of sin seen at a full light, undressed and unpainted, it were impossible, while it so appeared, that any one soul could be in love with it."—*Leighton.*

24. *"The bread of God is He which cometh down from heaven, and giveth life unto the world.   Then said they unto Him, Lord, evermore give us this bread."*—JOHN vi. 33, 34.

"Be Christ our pattern and our guide,
His image may we bear :
Oh may we tread His holy steps,
His joy and glory share !"—
Enfield.

"A Christian is the highest style of man."—*Young.*

25. "*His name shall be called Wonderful, Counsellor, The Mighty God, The Everlasting Father, The Prince of Peace.*"—ISAIAH ix. 6.

> " Babe Jesus lay in Mary's lap ;
> The sun shone in His hair ;
> And so it was she saw, mayhap,
> The crown already there."

" I love to see this day well kept by rich and poor : it is a great thing to have one day in the year, at least, when you are sure of being welcome wherever you go, and of having, as it were, the world thrown open to you."—*Washington Irving.*

---

26. "*God hath tempered the body together, having given more abundant honour to that part which lacked: that there should be no schism in the body.*"—I CORINTHIANS xii. 24, 25.

> " By his own power were all things made ;
> By Him supported all things stand ;
> He is the whole creation's head,
> And angels fly at His command."—
> *Watts.*

" All that believe have the real UNITY ; which is most glorious, because inward and spiritual ; in the body, and to the head."—*Cromwell.*

---

27. "*And when they were come to the place which is called Calvary, there they crucified Him. Then said Jesus, Father, forgive them; for they know not what they do. And the people stood beholding.*"—LUKE xxiii. 33, 34, 35.

> " And ever since, that countenance
> Is on my pathway shining ;
> A sun from out a higher sky
> Whose light knows no declining."

" It were easier to untwist all the beams of light in the sky, separating and expunging one of the colours, than to get the character of Jesus, which is the real Gospel, out of the world."—*Bushnell.*

28. *" Accept, I beseech Thee, the free-will offerings of my mouth, O Lord, and teach me thy judgments."*—PSALM cxix, 108.

> " In truth my sacrifice is nothing worth,
> Yet Thou in mercy wilt not cast it forth ;
> Thou'lt put me not to shame, but for love's sake
> My offering take."

" Our heart has made to Thee its entreaty ; our lips have uttered their praise ; our minds have exercised themselves in things too hard for us, wert not Thou our Teacher? Accept our offerings ; bless our efforts."—*Lynch.*

29. *" God is a spirit: and they that worship Him must worship Him in spirit and in truth."*—JOHN iv. 24.

> " Bright King of Glory, blessed God,
> Our spirits bow before Thy seat ;
> To Thee we lift our humble thoughts,
> And worship at thine holy feet."

" Morality is good, and is accepted of God, as far as it goes ; but the difficulty is, it does not go far enough."—*Beecher.*

30. *" The name of the Lord is a strong tower; the righteous runneth into it, and is safe."*—PROVERBS xviii. 10.

> " Christ of all my hopes the ground,
> Christ, the spring of all my joy !
> Still in Thee let me be found,
> Still for Thee my powers employ."—
>
> *Windham.*

" In Him, the self-existent and infinite mind, the Christian beholds unceasingly an object of boundless sublimity, grandeur, beauty, and loveliness."—*Dwight.*

31. *"And it came to pass, when Jesus had ended these say-ings the people were astonished at his doctrine."*—
MATTHEW vii. 28.

"Things of time have voices—speak and perish.
  Art and love speak—but their words must be
Like sighings of illimitable forests,
  And waves of an unfathomable sea."—

A. A. Proctor.

"God Himself prescribed our sacred types, and will in time disclose their purport."—*Klopstock.*

LONDON:
PRINTED BY WILLIAM CLOWES AND SONS,
STAMFORD STREET AND CHARING CROSS.

CPSIA information can be obtained at www.ICGtesting.com
Printed in the USA
BVOW01s1631240114

342944BV00009BA/369/P